PENGUIN

A CHILD

HARRY CREWS was born in 1935 at the end of a dirt road in
Alma, Bacon County, Georgia, a rural community near the
Okefenokee Swamp. His father, a tenant farmer, died before
Harry was two years old. A mysterious childhood paralysis; a
horrible scalding accident; his mother's second, turbulent marriage and divorce from a drunken uncle whom Crews had been
led to believe was his natural father; and a move to Jacksonville,
Florida, for his mother to find factory work were experiences
that would feed his desire to imagine and, ultimately, to write.
As a teen, Crews served a tour in the Marine Corps. On the GI
Bill, Crews attended the University of Florida, where he earned
a bachelor's degree in literature followed by a master's in education, with which he taught high-school and junior-college
English. A protégé of Southern novelist Andrew Lytle, Crews
published his first short story in the *Sewanee Review* in 1963.
He published his first novel, *The Gospel Singer*, in 1968. Its publication earned Crews a new teaching job at the University of
Florida and paved the way for the publication of seven more
novels over the next eight years, including *Naked in Garden
Hills* (1969); *Car* (1972); *The Hawk Is Dying* (1973), which was
adapted into a film released in 2006; *The Gypsy's Curse* (1974);
and the widely acclaimed *A Feast of Snakes* (1976). Crews's rep-
utation as a bold and daring new voice in Southern writing grew
during this time. In the 1970s, he wrote for popular magazines,
including a monthly column for *Esquire* and essays for *Playboy*,
and screenplays. In 1978, Crews's memoir of his youth, *A
Childhood: The Biography of a Place*, was published to endur-
ing acclaim. Two compilations of his nonfiction works, *Blood
and Grits* and *Florida Frenzy*, were issued in 1979 and 1982,
respectively. A decade of drug and alcohol abuse and creative
lapses ended in 1987 with the publication of his ninth novel, *All
We Need of Hell*. Crews retired from the classroom after teaching for thirty years at the University of Florida in Gainesville.
Crews, who died in 2012 at age seventy-six, was a prominent
writer in the literary genre known as Dirty South or Grit Lit,
notable for its bizarre characters, grotesque violence, and satirical surrealism. His artistic forebears include William Faulkner,

Flannery O'Connor, and Erskine Caldwell, but Crews remade Southern gothic in his own rough-hewn image in eighteen memorable novels, including *Karate Is a Thing of the Spirit* (1971), *The Knockout Artist* (1988), and *Body* (1990), dozens of riveting nonfiction pieces, and one of the finest memoirs in American literature. In 2002, the University of Georgia Libraries inducted Harry Crews into the Georgia Writers Hall of Fame.

TOBIAS WOLFF is the author of the novels *The Barracks Thief* and *Old School*, the memoirs *This Boy's Life* and *In Pharaoh's Army*, and the short story collections *In the Garden of the North American Martyrs*, *Back in the World*, and *The Night in Question*. His most recent collection of short stories, *Our Story Begins*, won The Story Prize for 2008. Other honors include the PEN/Malamud Award and the Rea Award—both for excellence in the short story—the Los Angeles Times Book Prize, and the PEN/Faulkner Award. He has also been the editor of *Best American Short Stories*, *The Vintage Book of Contemporary American Short Stories*, and *A Doctor's Visit: The Short Stories of Anton Chekhov*. His work appears regularly in *The New Yorker*, *The Atlantic*, *Harper's*, and other magazines and literary journals.

HARRY CREWS

A Childhood

THE BIOGRAPHY OF A PLACE

Foreword by
TOBIAS WOLFF

PENGUIN BOOKS

PENGUIN BOOKS

An imprint of Penguin Random House LLC
penguinrandomhouse.com

First published in the United States of America by Harper & Row Publishers 1978
Published with a foreword by Tobias Wolff in Penguin Books 2022

LIBRARY OF CONGRESS CATALOGING-IN-PUBLICATION DATA
Names: Crews, Harry, 1935–2012, author. | Wolff,
Tobias, 1945– writer of foreword.
Title: A childhood : the biography of a place / Harry Crews ;
foreword by Tobias Wolff.
Description: First edition. | New York : Penguin Books 2022. |
Series: Penguin classics
Identifiers: LCCN 2021029407 (print) | LCCN 2021029408 (ebook) |
ISBN 9780143135333 (paperback) | ISBN 9780525506768 (ebook)
Subjects: LCSH: Crews, Harry, 1935–2012—Childhood and youth. | Novelists,
American—20th century—Biography. | Bacon County (Ga.)—Biography. |
LCGFT: Autobiographies.
Classification: LCC PS3553.R46 Z46 2022 (print) |
LCC PS3553.R46 (ebook) | DDC 813/.54 [B]—dc23
LC record available at https://lccn.loc.gov/2021029407
LC ebook record available at https://lccn.loc.gov/2021029408

Printed in the United States of America
3rd Printing

Set in Sabon LT Std

This book was written for my boy,
Byron Jason Crews

Survival is triumph enough.
—DAVID SHELLEY, IN CONVERSATION

Contents

A CHILDHOOD

Foreword

To enter this book is to enter another world. Though set in an American state—Georgia—in a time not so distant from our own—the first half of the twentieth century—any temptation to feel ourselves on familiar ground is continually revealed as illusion. The way of life Harry Crews describes here, its culture, relation to the land, its employments, trials, pleasures, and dangers—dangers that he himself barely survived—forbids the comfort of recognition. At times, but for the distinctive American music of the voices Crews records, and the occasional mention of a truck or tractor, we might well imagine ourselves in feudal Europe, or the Russia of serfdom. Or, given the eruptions of interfamily violence begetting revenge begetting more violence, Sicily. His past is indeed another country.

A word about those tractors. They figure as a distant rumor—we never see one, any more than we see the owners of the exhausted, unyielding land farmed by Crews's family and their neighbors. Those who plow these fields do so with the help of mules, if they're lucky enough to own one. Crews's father was not so lucky. He had to harness himself to the plow, make a mule of himself from sunup to sundown. Worn out by the labor, he died at thirty-three, leaving his family destitute.

"Wounds or scars," Crews writes, "give an awesome credibility to a story." He himself bore enough of these to support any number of stories. And so, it is clear, did the people he grew up with, their lives scarred by poverty and violence. In the absence of effective legal authority, they were left to settle their differences without official mediation or constraint. Indeed, recourse to the sheriff defined a man as a weakling, destined "to be brutalized and savaged endlessly." Crews witnessed violence in his own home, and felt it like a pulse in the society around him, brought on by causes great and trivial: "As many men have been killed over bird dogs and fence lines in South Georgia as anything else." His stepfather, in a drunken rage with Crews's mother, blew the mantel off their fireplace with a shotgun, and the night might well have come to a worse ending. "I knew for certain," he writes, "that it was not unusual for a man to shoot at his wife."

Crews does not use the word "poverty" to describe the conditions of his upbringing, perhaps because it is a word generally understood in relation to the prosperity of others—that is, as deprivation. Little as his family had, their community was hardly better off. They did not see themselves as particularly disadvantaged. And in extremity they could draw for a time on the slender resources of extended family or friends. But in truth their lives were a struggle for survival, so desperate at times that "being alive was like being awake in a nightmare." Their weight went up or down according to the season. The children were subject to rickets, and worms nesting in their throats had to be pulled out by hand to keep them from choking. The family could not afford misfortune, yet misfortune haunted them. When Crews's mother saw their two precious yearling calves headed toward a barrel of pesticide and ran out to intercept them, Crews, then a toddler, seized that moment of freedom to taste some raw lye his mother had been using to scrub the floor. His cries sent her running back to the house, and from there eight miles by cart to the doctor. When they finally got home again the two calves were dead, lying stiff by the barrel of poison. "The world that circumscribed the people I come from," Crews writes, "had so little margin for error, for bad luck, that when something went wrong, it almost always brought something else down with it."

Crews's family was not alone in their struggle to survive; and just as your misfortune could inspire generosity in friends and neighbors, it could also leave you vulnerable to abuse by other desperate souls. And there was plenty of desperation to go around. On the day Crews's father was buried, a thief sneaked into their smokehouse and stole the meat the family had stored there, all but one small piece—overlooked, or perhaps a grudging concession to the distant whisper of his conscience. They knew who had done it—the thief was a friend, and not only a friend, but a *close* friend. After such knowledge, what forgiveness? Yet Crews, understanding all too well the circumstances that could lead to such a damnable act, cannot bring himself to damn the man for it, or even to name him in this book of names, names repeated so lovingly they take on the weight of poetry.

Cecil.

Willalee.

Miss Emily.

Ora.

Alton.

Lottie Mae.

Tweek.

Indeed, the refusal to name the thief can be understood as a punishment as well as a mercy. But it is a mercy. "It was a hard time in that land, and a lot of men did things for which they were ashamed and suffered for the rest of their lives. But they did them because of hunger and sickness and because they could not bear the spectacle of their children dying from lack of a doctor and their wives growing old before they were thirty."

Hunger, sickness, accidental maiming, unremitting labor for the unreliable reward of another meal, violence, early death. Harry Crews works from a dark palette here, as the truth of his sometimes terrible experience demands, yet the great picture he paints is shot through with light and love, and without even the faintest tincture of bitterness or self-pity. In fact, he is grateful for what he sees as the good fortune of growing up where he did, among the people of that place—a feeling sharpened in him by his forced departure when his mother, in flight from her shotgun-wielding second husband, moved her small family to Florida to take a job in a cigar-rolling factory, and Crews finally encountered modernity. Refrigerators and flush toilets, but the air loud with engine noise, and greasy with exhaust. Houses crowded close together, but inhabited by distant strangers rather than old friends and kinfolk. Paved roads everywhere, but no fields, no mules plowing a furrow "with lovely exactitude." Dogs roaming the streets, but none herding cattle, or wrestling a sick cow to the ground to receive a dose of medicine.

Crews's sense of displacement affects us as well, touching us with his own nostalgia for the life he had to leave behind, ugly and hard as it sometimes was. "I come from people," he writes, "who believe the *home place* is as vital and necessary as the beating of your own heart. . . . It is your anchor in the world, that place, along with the memory of your kinsmen at the long supper table every night and the knowledge that it would always exist, if nowhere but in memory."

I give thanks for that memory of his, as I give thanks for the consummate art, and the great heart, that produced this beautiful book, now and forever part of my own memory, where I too have a seat at that long table, drinking in the stories.

TOBIAS WOLFF

PART 1

CHAPTER 1

My first memory is of a time ten years before I was born, and the memory takes place where I have never been and involves my daddy whom I never knew. It was the middle of the night in the Everglades swamp in 1925, when my daddy woke his best friend Cecil out of a deep sleep in the bunkhouse just south of the floating dredge that was slowly chewing its way across the Florida Peninsula from Miami on the Atlantic to Naples on the Gulf of Mexico, opening a route and piling dirt for the highway that would come to be known as the Tamiami Trail. The night was dark as only a swamp can be dark and they could not see each other there in the bunkhouse. The rhythmic stroke of the dredge's engine came counterpoint to my daddy's shaky voice as he told Cecil what was wrong.

When Cecil finally did speak, he said: "I hope it was good, boy. I sho do."

"What was good?"

"That Indian. You got the clap."

But daddy had already known. He had thought of little else since it had become almost impossible for him to give water because of the fire that started in his stomach and felt like it burned through raw flesh every time he had to water off. He had thought from sunup to dark of the chickee where he had lain under the palm roof being eaten alive by swarming mosquitoes as he rode the flat-faced Seminole girl, whose name he never knew and who grunted like a sow and smelled like something shot in the woods.

He had not wanted her, but they had been in the swamp for three years. They worked around the clock, and if they weren't working or sleeping, their time was pretty much spent drinking or fighting or shooting gators. So since he could not have what he wanted, he tried to want what he could have, but it had been miserable, all of it because of the way she sounded and the way she smelled and the mosquitoes clotted about their faces thick as a veil and the heavy black flies that crawled over their legs.

"It weren't all that good," daddy said.

"No," said Cecil, "I don't reckon it's ever *that* good."

Gonorrhea was a serious hurt in the days before they had penicillin, and the hurt was compounded because daddy had resisted getting any treatment or even telling anybody until the pain finally forced him to do it.

"I don't know what I'm gone do."

"I do," Cecil said. "We gotta get out of the swamp and find you a doctor."

Cecil felt some obligation to help, not only because they had been friends since childhood but also because it was Cecil who had left Bacon County first to work on the trail and was later able to get his buddy a job working with him. It was all in the best tradition of "If you git work, write." And when Cecil wrote that there was steady work and good pay to be had in the Everglades, Ray had followed him down there.

He got on one of the gangs cutting right-of-way and in less than two years worked his way into the job of dredge operator. He was then not yet twenty and it was a sweet accomplishment for a boy who had no education, who was away from the farm for the first time in his life. But the clap soured the whole thing considerably.

Cecil was waiting for him when he came out of the doctor's office in the little town of Arcadia, Florida. It was the third doctor daddy had seen, and this one agreed with the other two. The word was final.

"He says I got to do it."

"Jesus," Cecil said.

"It's no other way."

"You gone do it?"

"I don't see no other way. Everyone I seen says I got to have one taken off. I guess I do if it ain't no other way."

"Jesus."

On the long drive back to the swamp in Cecil's Model T Ford in the shimmering heat of early summer, they didn't talk. Daddy did say one thing. "I won't ever have any children if they take it off. That's what the doctors said. All three of'm said it."

Cecil didn't say anything.

Did what I have set down here as memory actually happen? Did the two men say what I have recorded, think what I have said they thought? I do not know, nor do I any longer care. My knowledge of my daddy came entirely from the stories I have been told about him, stories told me by my mother, by my brother, who was old enough when he died to remember him first hand, by my other kin people, and by the men and women who knew him while he was alive.

It is demonstrably true that he went to work on the Tamiami Trail when he was seventeen and worked there until he was twenty-three. He did get the clap down there and he did lose a testicle because of it in the little town of Arcadia. He came back to Bacon County with money in his pocket and a gold watch inscribed on the back: "To Ray Crews, Pioneer Builder of the Tamiami Trail." Cecil got such a watch, as did several of the men who saw the job through from start to finish. Those are facts, but the rest of it came down to me through the mouths of more people than I could name. And I have lived with the stories of him for so long that they are as true as anything that ever actually happened to me. They are true because I think they are true. I, of course, had no alternative. It would have been impossible for me to think otherwise.

Jean-Paul Sartre in his autobiography *Words*, when writing about a man's tendency to smother his son, said his own father sired him and then had the decency to die. I've always thought that because my daddy died before I could ever know him, he became a more formidable memory, a greater influence, and a more palpable presence than he would ever have been had he lived. I'm not sure precisely what that says about me, but surely it must say more about me than it does about my daddy or his death. It also says a great deal about the people and the place I come from. Nothing is allowed to die in a society of storytelling people. It is all—the good and the bad—carted up and brought along from one generation to the next. And everything that is brought along is colored and shaped by those who bring it.

If that is so, is what they bring with them true? I'm convinced that it is. Whatever violence may be done to the letter of their collective experience, the spirit of that experience remains intact and true. It is their notion of themselves, their understanding of who they are. And it was just for this reason that I started this book, because I have never been certain of who *I* am.

I have always slipped into and out of identities as easily as other people slip into and out of their clothes. Even my voice, its inflections and rhythms, does not seem entirely my own. On journalism assignments during which I've recorded extended interviews with politicians or film stars or truck drivers my own voice will inevitably become almost indistinguishable from the voice of the person with whom I'm talking by the third or fourth tape. Some natural mimic in me picks up whatever verbal tics or mannerisms it gets close to. That mimic in myself has never particularly pleased me, has in fact bothered me more than a little.

But whatever I am has its source back there in Bacon County, from which I left when I was seventeen years old to join the Marine Corps, and to which I never returned to live. I have always known, though, that part of me never left, could never leave, the place where I was born and, further, that what has been most significant in my life had all taken place by the time I was six years old. The search for those six years inevitably led me first to my daddy's early life and early death. Consequently, I have had to rely not only on my own memory but also on the memory of others for what follows here: the biography of a childhood which necessarily is the biography of a place, a way of life gone forever out of the world.

On a blowing March day in 1927, just before his twenty-third birthday, my daddy started back home with his friend Cecil in the Model T Ford. They had been down in the swamp for six years, though, and they were in no particular hurry. With a bottle of whiskey between them on the floorboard, it took nearly three weeks to make the 500 miles up the coast of Florida on U.S. Highway 1, a blacktop double-lane that followed the edge of the ocean up from Miami to Fort Pierce to Daytona and on to Jacksonville. From Jacksonville, they cut up toward the St. Marys River, which divides Florida from Georgia. The air went heavy with the smell of turpentine and pine trees as they drove on north through Folkston and Waycross and finally through Alma, a town of dirt streets, a cotton gin, a warehouse, two grocery stores, a seed and fertilizer store, and a doctor, who had—besides a cash register—some pens out back to hold his fees when they came in the form of chickens and goats and hogs.

In the car with him as they drove, there was a shoebox full of pictures of my daddy with five or six of his buddies, all of them holding whiskey bottles and pistols and rifles and coons and leashed alligators out there in the rugged dug-out sea of saw grass and mangrove swamp through which they had built the Tamiami Trail.

As I work, I have those pictures, yellowed now, still in a pasteboard shoebox where they have always been kept. For better than four decades, when the old shoebox wore out every year or so, the pictures have gone into a new shoebox. I once put them in a heavy leather album, the better to keep them, I thought. But after a week or so, I took them out again. The album seemed wrong. I did not like to look at them caught in the stiff, protected pages. I gave no thought to why I didn't like to see them there, but I believe now it was because a worn and vulnerable pasteboard box more accurately reflected my tenuous connection with him whom I never knew but whose presence has never left me, has always followed me just out of reach and hailing distance like some vague, half-realized shadow.

Looking at them, I think I see some of what my daddy was and some of what I have become. He was taller than I have ever grown, being as he was six feet two and weighing always about 170 pounds. Everything about him—the way he stands, his every gesture—suggests a man of endless and exuberant energy, a man who believes in his bones that anything worth doing is worth overdoing. His is the gun that is always drawn;

his is the head that is turned back under the whiskey bottle. He has already had enough trouble and sickness and loss in his short life to have broken a lesser man, but there is more often than not a smile of almost maniacal joy, a smile stretched around a mouthful of teeth already loosened by pyorrhea, a disease which would take the two front teeth out of the top gum before he died shortly after my birth.

They made their way up the coast of Florida, stopping here and there, staying at one place in Jacksonville for nearly a week, drinking and being rowdy in the best way of young men who have been on a hard job and now have money in their pockets, always talking, rehashing again what they had done and where they had been and where they were going and what they hoped for themselves and their families, even though my daddy carried with him the sure and certain knowledge that he would never have any children.

"It ain't the worst thing that could happen," Cecil said. "You ain't but a partial gelding."

"That ain't real funny, Cecil."

"I reckon not. But it still ain't the worst thing."

They were on the St. Marys River in a rented rowboat, drifting, drinking, ignoring the bobbing corks at the ends of their lines, not caring whether they caught anything or not after six years in a swamp where fish had been as plentiful as mosquitoes.

Daddy said: "If it ain't the worst thing, it'll do till the worst thing comes along."

Cecil gave his slow drunken smile, a smile at once full of kidding and love. "The worst thing woulda been to let that old man and his boy eat you alive."

"They'd a had to by God do it."

"Oh, they'd a done it all right. They'd already et several before they started looking at how tender you was."

"I guess. Dying cain't be all that hard though. Without thinking about it at all, people drop dead right and left."

Cecil said: "It's one thing to drop dead. It's sumpin else to have your head pulled off."

These were not violent men, but their lives were full of

violence. When daddy first went down to the Everglades, he started on a gang that cut the advance right-of-way and, consequently, was out of the main camp for days, at times for more than a week. When he almost got killed working out there on the gang, Cecil almost killed a man because of it. Daddy's foreman was an old man, grizzled, stinking always of chewing tobacco and sweat and whiskey, and known throughout the construction company as a man mean as a bee-stung dog. He didn't have to dislike you to hurt you, even cripple you. He just liked to hurt and cripple, and he had a son that was very much his daddy's boy.

Because my daddy was only seventeen when he went out there, the full fury of their peculiar humor fell upon him, so much so that once it almost cost him a leg in what was meant to look like an accident when a cable snapped. If it had only been some sort of initiation rite, it would have one day ended. But daddy was under a continual hazing that was meant to draw blood.

When he got back to camp, he found Cecil over by the mess wagon. When he'd finished eating, daddy said: "I'm scared, Cecil. That old man and his boy's gone kill me."

Cecil was still at his beans. "He ain't gone kill you."

"I think he means to."

Cecil put his plate down and said: "No, he ain't cause you and me's gone settle it right now."

Cecil was six feet seven inches tall and weighed between 250 and 275 pounds depending upon the season of the year.

"Cecil, that old man don't know how strong he is his own self."

"He's about to find out. You just keep his boy off me. I'll take care of the old man."

They found the old man and his boy on the dredge and the fight was as short as it was brutal. They locked up and went off the dredge into the mud, the old man on the bottom but with his hands locked on Cecil's throat. He would have killed him, too, if Cecil had not thought to provide himself with a ten-inch steel ringbolt in the back pocket of his overalls which he used to break the old man's skull. But even with his head cracked, it took two men to get his hands from around Cecil's throat.

The old man was taken out to a hospital in Miami and his boy, whom daddy had managed to mark superficially, a cut across his forehead and another down the length of his back, went with him and nothing more was heard of the matter. At least for the moment. But a little over two months later word came into the swamp that the old man and his boy were coming back.

"Me and Luther's comin back to settle. We gone take the big-uns one by one and the littluns two by two."

Cecil sent word back on a piece of ruled tablet paper. "If you and that boy come out here for me and Ray, have your boxes built and ready. You gone need'm before you git out again."

For whatever reason, the old man and his boy did not come back into the swamp. The matter had been settled. Surely not to everybody's satisfaction, but settled nonetheless. They had done it themselves without recourse to law or courts. That was not unusual for them and their kind.

Up in Jeff Davis County, just about where I was born and raised, a woman's husband was killed and she—seven months pregnant—was the only witness to the killing. When the sheriff tried to get her to name the man who'd done it, she only pointed to her swelling stomach and said: "He knows who did it, and when the time comes, he will settle it." And that was all she ever said.

In Bacon County, the sheriff was the man who tried to keep the peace, but if you had any real trouble, you did not go to him for help to make it right. You made it right yourself or else became known in the county as a man who was defenseless without the sheriff at his back. If that ever happened, you would be brutalized and savaged endlessly because of it. Men killed other men oftentimes not because there had been some offense that merited death, but simply because there had been an offense, any offense. As many men have been killed over bird dogs and fence lines in South Georgia as anything else.

Bacon County was that kind of place as they drove into it finally toward the middle of March in 1927. There were very few landowners. Most people farmed on shares or standing rent. Shares meant the owner would supply the land, fertilizer, seed, mules, harness, plows, and at harvest take half of everything that was made. On standing rent, you agreed to pay the landowner a certain sum of money for the use of the land. He took nothing but the money. Whether on shares or on standing rent, they were still tenant farmers and survival was a day-to-day crisis as real as rickets in the bones of their children or the worms that would sometimes rise out of their children's stomachs and nest in their throats so that they had to be pulled out by hand to keep the children from choking.

The county itself was still young then, having been formed in 1914 and named for Senator Augustus Octavius Bacon, who was born in Bryan County and lived out much of his life in the city of Macon. Bacon County is as flat as the map it's drawn on and covered with pine trees and blackjack oak and sand ridges and a few black gum and bay trees down in the bottomland near running creeks. Jeff Davis and Appling counties are to the north of it, Pierce and Coffee counties to the east, and the largest county in the state, Ware, joins its southern border.

There was a section of Bacon County famous all over Georgia for moonshining and bird dogs and violence of one kind or another. It was called Scuffletown, not because it was a town or even a crossroads with a store in it, but because as everybody said: "They always scuffling up there." Sometimes the scuffling was serious; sometimes not.

About a month before my daddy drove back into the county, Jay Scott opened his mouth once too often to a man named Junior "Bad Eye" Carter. He was called Bad Eye because he was putting up wire fence as a young man and the staple he was driving into the post glanced off the hammer and drove itself deep into his right eye. He rode a mule all the way to Alma, where the doctor pulled out the staple, but the eye was gone forever. Having only a left eye gave him an intense, even crazy stare. Talk was that he could conjure with that unblinking, staring left eye.

For a long time there had been bad blood between Bad Eye and Jay Scott over a misunderstanding about some hogs. Bad

Eye was chopping wood for the stove when Jay walked up. The woodpile was just inside the wire fence that ran along the public road. Jay stopped in the road and for a long time just watched him. But finally, watching wasn't enough.

"Watch out, old man, a splinter don't fly up there and put out that other eye."

Bad Eye kept on chopping, the strokes of the ax regular as clock ticking. He never even looked up.

"Splinter in that other eye, we'd have to call you Bad *Face*."

Ruby, Bad Eye's wife, saw the whole thing from the water shelf on the back porch of the house where she was standing. Jay saw Ruby on the back porch and said, loud enough for her to hear: "Why don't you git your old woman out here? They tell me she does most of the ax work for you anyhow."

That was when Bad Eye looked up, a big vein standing in his forehead. "You stand out there in a public road and talk all you want to. But don't come over the fence onto my land. Don't reckon you'd have the stomach for that, would you?"

Jay came across the ditch, put one foot in the wire and one hand on top of the fence post, getting ready to climb up and swing over. But he never did. That was as far as he got. Bad Eye, who had started chopping again, never missed a stroke, but drove the blade of the ax through Jay's wrist and two inches deep into the top of the post. Ruby said she bet you could hear him scream for five miles. Said she bet somebody thought they was slaughtering hogs, late in the year as it was.

Jay tied off his arm with his belt and then fainted in the ditch. When he woke up, Bad Eye was sitting on the woodpile with the bloody stump of a hand.

"This here hand belongs to me now, sumbitch. Found it on my land."

Jay fainted again. Two of Bad Eye Carter's kinsmen were killed in the fight to get the hand back. Jay wanted to give it a Christian burial. They never did get it back, but Bad Eye went fishing one day and didn't come back. They finally found him floating in Little Satilla River. His blue and wrinkled body had raised the fifty pounds of rusty plow points tied about his ankles.

It was this part of the county that my daddy and his people came from, back up in what's known as the Forks of the Hurricane, not far from Cartertown, which was not a town either but simply a section of the county where almost every farmer was named Carter. The Forks of the Hurricane was where two wide creeks rose in Big Hurricane Swamp and flowed out across the county, one creek called Little Hurricane and the other Big Hurricane. I was a grown man before I realized that the word we were saying was *hurricane* because it was universally pronounced harrikin.

So daddy came back to the home place, where his own daddy, Dan, and his mama, Lilly, lived with their family, a family which, like most families then, was big. His brothers and sisters were named Vera, D.W., Bertha, Leroy—who was crippled from birth—Melvin, Ora, Pascal, and Audrey.

Daddy's granddaddy had once been a slave owner and a large landholder, but his family, like most families in that time and place, had fallen on evil days. They still owned the land they lived on, but they had to constantly fight the perpetual mortgage held by the bank. There was a place to put your head down and usually enough to eat, but when daddy came home from the swamp, farmers were saying there wasn't enough cash money in the county to close up a dead man's eyes.

Daddy proceeded to do what so many young men have done before him, that is, if not to make a fool of himself, at least to behave so improvidently that he ran through what little money he'd been able to get together working in Florida. Cecil drove off to live in the mountains of North Georgia, so daddy bought himself a Model T Ford and he bought his mama a piano and he bought himself a white linen suit and a white wide-brimmed hat. I don't know how he could have managed it after the car and the piano, but he may have bought himself several of those white suits, judging from the number of pictures I have of him dressed in one. In the first flower of his manhood, he was a great poser for pictures, always with a young lady and sometimes with several young ladies.

I lift the lid off the shoebox now and reach in. The first picture I see is of him, his foot propped up on the running board of his Model T Ford, standing there with a young lady wearing her bonnet, the sun in their faces, smiling. And looking into his face is like looking into my own. His cheekbones are high and flat, and a heavy ridge of bone casts a perpetual shadow over his eyes. There is a joy and great confidence in the way he stands, his arm around the girl, a cock-of-the-walk tilt to his pelvis. And along with that photograph there are others: him sitting under a tree with another young lady, she short-haired and wearing a brimless little hat almost like a cap; him leaning against the front fender of the Model T, still in that immaculate white linen suit with yet another young lady; him standing between two girls in their Sunday frocks on the bank of a river, probably the Little Hurricane.

There is no doubt that in that time he was, as they say in Bacon County, fond of lying out with dry cattle. Maidens, or at least those young ladies who had never had a child, were called dry cattle after the fact that a cow does not give milk until after giving birth to a calf. An unflattering way to refer to women, God knows, but then those were unflattering times.

He was also bad to go to the bottle, as so many men have been in the family. He drank his whiskey and lay out with dry cattle and stayed in the woods at night running foxes and talking and laughing with his friends and was vain enough to have it recorded as often as he could with somebody's camera. It must have been a good time for him then, a time when he did not yet have a wife and children or the obligations that always come with them.

Because of the stories I've heard about him, his recklessness, his tendency to stay up all night and stay in the woods when he probably should have been doing something else, and his whiskey drinking, I have often wondered if in some way that he could not or would not have said, he felt his own early death just around the bend. He had been an extremely sickly child and Granddaddy Dan Crews had never thought that he would raise him to manhood. When daddy was three years old, he got rheumatic fever and from it developed what they called then a leaking heart. After he developed the trouble with his heart, apparently from the fever, his kidneys did not work the way they should and he would swell up from fluid retention and spent much of his childhood either sitting in a chair or half reclining on a bed.

The doctors in Baxley and Blackshear and even as far away as Waycross—about thirty-five miles—had been unable to help him. Granddaddy Dan in desperation mailed off for some pills he saw advertised in the almanac. Daddy's brother, Uncle Melvin, told me that when the medicine came, the pills were as big as a quarter, the size you might try on a horse. Granddaddy Dan took one look at them and decided he couldn't give them to his boy as little and sick as he was. So he put them on the crosspiece up over the door and forgot about them. But daddy, then only five years old, but already showing the hardheaded willfulness that would follow him through his short life, began to take the pills without anybody knowing about it. Whether it was the pills or the grace of God, the swelling began to go down and within a month he was able to get out in the field and hoe a little bit and in the coming weeks he gradually got better.

But he always had that murmur in his heart. Mama says she could hear it hissing and skipping when she lay with him at night, her head on his chest, and it was that hissing, skipping heart which eventually killed him. That and his predisposition to hurt himself. There seemed to be something in him then and later, a kind of demon, madness even, that drove him to work too hard, to carouse the same way, and always to be rowdier than was good for him.

Maybe it was his conviction that he would never have children that was hurting him, doing bad things in his head and making him behave as he did. He had to have thought of it often and it had to give him pain. Families were important then, and they were important not because the children were useful in the fields to break corn and hoe cotton and drop potato vines in wet weather or help with hog butchering and all the rest of it. No, they were important because a large family was the only thing a man could be sure of having. Nothing else was certain. If a man had no education or even if he did, the hope of putting money in the bank and keeping it there or owning a big piece of land free and clear, such hope was so remote that few men ever let themselves think about it. The timber in the county was of no consequence, and there was very little rich bottomland. Most of the soil was poor and leached out, and commercial fertilizer was dear as blood. But a man didn't need good land or stands of hardwood trees to have babies. All he needed was balls and the inclination.

And in that very fact, the importance of family, lies what I think of as the rotten spot at the center of my life or, said another way, the rotten spot at the center of what my life might have been if circumstances had been different. I come from people who believe the *home place* is as vital and necessary as the beating of your own heart. It is that single house where you were born, where you lived out your childhood, where you grew into young manhood. It is your anchor in the world, that place, along with the memory of your kinsmen at the long supper table every night and the knowledge that it would always exist, if nowhere but in memory.

Such a place is probably important to everybody everywhere, but in Bacon County—although nobody to my knowledge ever said it—the people understand that if you do not have a home place, very little will ever be yours, really *belong* to you in the world. Ever since I reached manhood, I have looked back upon that time when I was a boy and thought how marvelous beyond saying it must be to spend the first ten or fifteen years of your life in the same house—the *home* place—moving among the same furniture, seeing on the familiar walls the same pictures of blood kin. And more marvelous still, to be able to return to that place of your childhood and see it through the eyes of a man, with everything you see set against that long-ago, little boy's memory of how things used to be.

But because we were driven from pillar to post when I was a child, there is nowhere I can think of as the home place. Bacon County is my home place, and I've had to make do with it. If I think of where I come from, I think of the entire county. I think of all its people and its customs and all its loveliness and all its ugliness.

CHAPTER 2

Being as impermanent as the wind, constantly moving, I lost track for thirty-five years of my daddy's side of the family. I remember nothing specific of my paternal grandparents, and my paternal aunts and uncles remained strangers until I was grown. It was not their fault, nor was it mine or anyone else's. It just happened that way.

I saw a good deal of the kin on my mama's side. My Uncle Alton, her brother, was as much as any other man a father to me. He's dead now, but I will always carry a memory of him in my heart as vivid as any memory I have.

I was sitting on the steps of his front porch just after I got out of the Marine Corps in 1956, when I was twenty-one years old, watching him smoking one hand-rolled Prince Albert cigarette after another and spitting between his feet into the yard. He was so reticent that if he said a sentence ten words long, it seemed as though he had been talking all afternoon.

He was probably the closest friend of the longest standing that my daddy ever had. And I remember sitting there on the steps, looking up at him in his rocking chair and talking about my daddy, saying that I thought the worst thing that had happened in my life was his early death, that never having known him, I knew that I would, one way or another, be looking for him the rest of my life.

"What is it you want to know?" he said.

"I don't know what I want to know," I said. "Anything. Everything."

"Cain't know everything," he said. "And anything won't help."

"I think it might," I said. "Anything'll help me see him better than I see him now. At least I'd have some notion of him."

He watched me for a moment with his steady gray eyes looking out from under the brim of the black felt hat he always wore and said: "Let's you and me take us a ride."

He started for the pickup truck parked in the lane beyond the yard and I followed. As was his way, he didn't say where we were going and I didn't ask. It was enough for me to be riding with him over the flat dirt roads between walls of black pine trees on the way to Alma. He lived then about three miles from the Little Satilla River which separates Bacon from Appling County and very near two farms that I had lived on as a boy. We drove the twelve miles to the paved road that led into town, but shortly after we turned into it, he stopped at a little grocery store with Pepsi-Cola and root beer and Redman Chewing Tobacco and snuff signs nailed all over it and two gas pumps out front in the red clay lot where several pickup trucks were parked.

We got down and went in. Some men were sitting around in the back of the store on nail kegs and ladder-back chairs or squatting on their heels, apparently doing nothing very much but smoking and chewing and talking.

One of them came to the front where we had stopped by the counter. "How you, Alton?" he said.

Uncle Alton said: "We all right. Everything all right with you, Joe?"

"Jus fine, I reckon. What can I git you?"

"I guess you can let us have two of them cold Co-Colers."

The man got two Cokes out of the scarred red box behind him and Uncle Alton paid him. We went on back to where the men were talking. They all spoke to Uncle Alton in the brief and easy way of men who had known each other all their lives.

They spoke for a while about the weather, mostly rain, and about other things that men who live off the land speak of when they meet, seriously, but with that resigned tone in their voice that makes you know they know they're speaking only to pass the time because they have utterly no control over what they're talking about: weevils in cotton, screwworms in stock, the government allotment of tobacco acreage, the fierce price of commercial fertilizer.

We hadn't been there long before Uncle Alton said casually, as though it were something that had just occurred to him: "This is Ray Crews' boy. Name Harry."

The men turned and looked at me for a long considered time and it again seemed the most natural thing in the world for them to now begin talking about my daddy, who had been dead for more than twenty years. I didn't know it then and didn't even know it or realize it for a long time afterward, but what Uncle Alton had done, because of what I'd said to him on the porch, was take me out in the truck to talk with men who had known my father.

Maybe the men themselves knew it, or maybe they simply liked my father in such a way that the mention of his name was enough to bring back stories and considerations of people who were kin to him. Without making any special thing out of it they began to talk about those days when daddy was a boy, about how many children were in his family, and then about how families were not as big now as they once had been and from that went on to talk about my grandma's sister, Aunt Belle, who had fourteen children, all of whom lived to be grown, and finally to the time one of Aunt Belle's boys, Orin Bennett, was killed at a liquor still by a government man.

"Well," one of them said, "it's a notion most people have nowadays moonshinin was easy work, but it weren't."

"Moonshinin was hard work. Real hard work."

"Most men I known back in them days," said Uncle Alton, "made moonshine because it weren't nothing else to do. They'as working at the only thing it was to work at. I feel like most folks who make shine even today do it for the same reason."

"I'll tell you sumpin else," Joe said. "I never known men back then makin shine that thought it was anythin wrong with it. It was a livin, the only livin they had."

One of them looked at me and said: "It wasn't much whiskey made in your daddy's family, though. I don't know the ins and outs of how Orin come to be killed up at that there still.

But your granddaddy didn't hold with none of his own young-uns making whiskey or bein anywhere around where it was made. Not ole Dan Crews didn't. He'd take a drink, drunk his full share, I'd say, but he never thought makin it was proper work for a man."

"I've made some and I've drunk some, and I'd shore a heap ruther drink it than make it."

Just as natural as spitting, a bottle of bonded whiskey out of which about a quarter had been drunk appeared from somewhere behind one of the chairs. The cap was taken off. The man who took it off wiped the neck of the bottle on his jumper sleeve, took a sip, and handed it to the man squatting beside him. The bottle passed. Uncle Alton, God love him, didn't have any of the whiskey. Even then his stomach, which finally killed him, was beginning to go bad on him.

The man who had done most of the talking since we came in finally looked up at me and said: "It'll take a lot of doing, son, to fill your daddy's shoes. He was much of a man."

I said: "I didn't think to fill'm. It's trouble enough trying to fill the ones I'm standing in."

For whatever reason they seemed to like that. One of them took a hit out of the bottle and leaned back on his nail keg and said: "Lemme tell you a story, son. It was a feller Fletchum, Tweek we called'm, Tweek Fletchum, and he musta been about twenty-seven years old then, but even that young he already had the name of makin the best whiskey in the county. Makin whiskey and mean enough to bite a snake to boot." He stopped long enough to shake his head over how mean ole Tweek was and also used the pause to bubble the whiskey bottle a couple of times. "Me and you daddy was hired out plowin for Luke Tate and one evenin after we took the mules out we decided to go on back there to Tweek's place to where his still was at. We weren't nothing but yearlin boys then, back before he went off to work down in Flardy, we couldn't a been much more'n six-teen years old, but we *would* touch a drop or two of whiskey from time to time.

"We didn't do a thing but cut back through the field and cross the branch and then up Ten Mile Creek past that place your daddy later tended for one of the Boatwright boys. When we got to Tweek's, his wife, Sarah, pretty thing, a Turner before she married Tweek, she seen us comin and met us at the door and said Tweek was back at the still and me'n your daddy started back there to where he was at. Tweek didn't keep nothin at his house but bonded whiskey an that was just for show in case some govment man come nosin around, so we went on back to the still and while we'as kickin along there in the dust, we decided to play us a little trick on Tweek. I cain't remember who thought it up, but it seem like to me it'as your daddy because he was ever ready for some kind of foolishness, playin tricks and such. That ain't sayin a thing agin him, it was just his nature. Coulda been me, though, that thought it up. Been known for such myself.

"Anyhow, that still of Tweek's was set right slap up agin Big Harrikin Swamp. Out in front of the still was the damnedest wall of brambles and briers you ever seen in your life. Musta been twenty acres of them thins, some of'm big as a scrub oak. And it was that suckhole swamp in back of the still. Brambles in front and waist-deep swamp full of moccasins in back, with a little dim woods road runnin in from one side and then runnin out the othern.

"Your daddy went around and come up the woods road from one side, and I went around and come up the other. Everybody was having trouble them days with that govment man come in here from Virginia or sommers like that and given everybody so much trouble before Lummy finally killed him, but in them days, Tweek and everybody else was having trouble with 'm, so when I was sure your daddy had time to git on the other side, I got up close to the still in a clump of them gallberry bushes and cupped my mouth like this, see here, and shouted into my shirt: 'STAY RIGHT THERE!'

"Tweek he was stirrin him some mash, but when I hollered, he taken and thrown down the paddle and jerked his head up like a dog cuttin a rank spoor in the woods. He tuck off runnin down the road the other way, his shirttail standin out flat behind him. I didn't do a thing but cup my mouth agin like this here and holler: 'HEAD'M OVER THERE!' And a course he was runnin straight at your daddy. He waited till ole Tweek got real close and then hollered: 'I GOT'M OVER HERE!'

"Tweek come up slidin soon's he known the road was closed on him at both ends and he tuck him a long look at the Harrikin Swamp behind him and then he tuck'm a long look at them brambles in front of him. And I got to credit ole Tweek, it didn't take'm but about three seconds to make his mind up. He put his head down and charged them briers and brambles.

"We heard'm screamin and thrashin around out there for what musta been fifteen minutes. It was as funny a thing as I ever hope to see, and damn if me and your daddy didn't bout break a rib settin there sippin some mash Tweek'd more'n likely run off that mornin, all the time listenin to Tweek out there screamin and tearin through the brambles.

"Got through and went on back up there to the house and Sarah said, 'No, Tweek ain't come in,' so we set down on the front porch swing to finish off that little mason fruit jar of shine we'd taken from the still. Well, it was damn nigh dark and we'd moved into the kitchen where we'as settin at the table, a kerosene lamp between us, eatin sausage and syrup that Sarah given us, when what do we hear but this te-nine-see *scratchin* at the back door.

"Sarah opened it and I could see Tweek standin down in the yard, but he didn't see us. He was cut from lap to lip, nothin but blood and scratches on his face and neck.

"'Sarah,' says Tweek, 'put a little sumpin in a sack to eat. Goddamned govment man's after me.'

"She says, 'Tweek, that weren't no govment man. Them's just Ray and Tom that. . . .'"

"But we didn't hear the rest of it cause we heard him beller like a bull and seen he was going for the shotgun. Onliest thing that saved us was he had bird shot in it and maybe on account of it was gitten on toward black dark. But he thrown down on us as we'as goin out the fence gate. Your daddy didn't catch none of it, but I'm carryin sign to this day."

He unbuckled his galluses and pulled up his work shirt. His back was full of little purple holes, like somebody had set it afire and then put the fire out with an ice pick.

Uncle Alton and I stayed around for three or four hours talking and drinking—or at least I was drinking a little—and listening to stories and talking about my daddy and his people.

I'd heard the moonshine story sitting around the fireplaces of a dozen different farms. This was the first time I'd ever heard that daddy was there when Tweek had two years of his growth scared out of him, but this was also the first time I ever had the storyteller lift his shirt and show me the sign of the bird shot. Wounds or scars give an awesome credibility to a story.

Listening to them talk, I wondered what would give credibility to my own story if, when my young son grows to manhood, he has to go looking for me in the mouths and memories of other people. Who would tell the stories? A few motorcycle riders, bartenders, editors, half-mad karateka, drunks, and writers. They are scattered all over the country, but even if he could find them, they could speak to him with no shared voice from no common ground. Even as I was gladdened listening to the stories of my daddy, an almost nauseous sadness settled in me, knowing I would leave no such life intact. Among the men with whom I have spent my working life, university professors, there is not one friend of the sort I was listening to speak of my daddy there that day in the back of the store in Bacon County. Acquaintances, but no friends. For half of my life I have been in the university, but never of it. Never *of* anywhere, really. Except the place I left, and that of necessity only in memory. It was in that moment and in that knowledge that I first had the notion that I would someday have to write about it all, but not in the convenient and comfortable metaphors of fiction, which I had been doing for years. It would have to be done naked, without the disguising distance of the third person pronoun. Only the use of *I*, lovely and terrifying word, would get me to the place where I needed to go.

In the middle of the afternoon, Uncle Alton and I left the store and drove out to New Lacy, a little crossroads village where Uncle Elsie and Aunt Gertie lived with their house full of children until Uncle Elsie died. Aunt Gertie was my mama's sister and Uncle Elsie spoke in tongues.

We sat on a little porch with a man who must have been old when daddy died. His eyes were solid and cloud-colored, and his skin so wrinkled and folded it looked like it might have been made for a man twice his size. His mouth was toothless and dark and worked continuously around a plug of tobacco as he told us about chickens with one wing and chickens with one leg gimping about over the first farm my daddy worked on shares.

"Mule was bad to bite chickens," he said, sending a powerful stream of tobacco juice into the yard, apparently without even stopping to purse his old wrinkled lips. "Been your daddy's mule he mought woulda killed it. Horse mule, he was, name of Sheddie."

The old man had withered right down to bone, but his mind was as sharp as a boy's.

"Workin shares like he was, Sheddie come with the crop. But he was bad to bite chickens like I said. Chicken'd hop up on the feed trough to peck a little corn and Sheddie'd just take him a bite. Sometimes he'd git a wing, sometimes a leg. Sometimes the whole damn chicken."

He began to cough and he stopped to spray the porch with black spit.

"Ray he got tired of seein all them chickens hobblin about the place with a wing or a leg missin. So he cured that Sheddie, he did."

Daddy, the old man said, killed a chicken and hung it up to ripen. When it was good and rotten, he blindfolded Sheddie, put on a halter with a jawbreaker bit, and fastened that stinking chicken to the bit with hay wire. It was a full day before the chicken came completely off the bit it had been wired to. Sheddie was never known to bite again. He had lost his taste for chicken.

Before we got through that afternoon, Uncle Alton and I had been all over Bacon County and never once had he said to anybody: "Here is Ray Crews' son and he never knew his daddy and he wants to hear about him." And yet, somehow, he contrived to have the stories told. We finally went back to his house a little after dark and he never mentioned that afternoon again to me nor I to him, but I'll always be grateful for it.

It was through his friendship with my Uncle Alton that daddy first took notice of my mama, whose name is Myrtice. I suppose it was inevitable that he eventually should, because in the same shoebox with his pictures—the pictures of him playing the dandy with half the girls of the county—is a picture of mama just before she turned sixteen. She is sitting in a pea patch, wearing a print dress. And even in the faded black-and-white photograph, you can tell she is round and pink and pretty as she smiles in a fetching way under a white bonnet.

As pretty as she was, though, God knows there were enough children in the family for her to get lost in the crowd. Besides Uncle Alton and mama there was Dorsey, who died when he was four years old from diphtheria. Then there was Aunt Ethel and Aunt Olive and Leon, who died of pneumonia when he was two, and Aunt Gertie and Uncle Frank and Uncle Harley and Aunt Lottie and Aunt Bessie. Grandma Hazelton, whose name was the same as Grandma Crews, Lilly, gave birth to children over a period of twenty years. Nine of them lived to be grown and married. As I write this today, three are still living.

I think he really noticed her for the first time the day her daddy, Grandpa Hazelton, almost killed a man with his walking stick. My daddy had come over to their place for the very reason that he knew there was going to be trouble. He could have saved himself the trip because as it turned out, Grandpa handled the whole thing very nicely and with considerable dispatch.

Uncle Alton, who had just turned seventeen at the time, had managed to get in a row with a man named Jessup over a shoat hog.

"Pa," Uncle Alton said, "Jessup says he's coming over here today and he's gone bring his friends with him."

Grandpa Hazelton was never a man to talk much, probably because he didn't hear very well. He said: "He ain't comin on the place and causin no trouble."

But they did, later that day, three grown men. They stood in the dooryard and called Uncle Alton out, saying they had brought a cowwhip and meant to mark him with it.

Grandpa Hazelton said: "You men git off my place. You on my land and Alton here ain't nothing but a boy. You all git off the place."

Daddy and Uncle Alton were standing on the porch with Grandpa when he said it. The three men, all of whom had been drinking, said they'd go when they got ready, but first they had business to take care of and they meant to do it.

There were no other words spoken. Grandpa Hazelton came off the porch carrying the heavy hickory walking stick he always had with him, a stick he carried years before he actually needed it. He hit the man who had spoken between the eyes with the stick, hit him so hard that his palate dropped in his mouth.

The two men carried their friend, his dropped palate bleeding and his tongue half choking him, to the wagon they had come in and headed off toward town for the doctor. Grandpa followed them all the way to the wagon, beating them about the head and shoulders with his stick.

He stood in the lane shaking with rage and told them: "You come back on the place, I got some buckshot for you."

In that time, a man's land was inviolate, and you were always very careful about what you said to another man if you were on his land. A man could shoot you with impunity if you were on his property and he managed to get you dead enough so you couldn't tell what actually happened. The sheriff would come, look around, listen to the man whose land the killing took place on, and then go back to town. That was that.

In the commotion of the fight, the whole Hazelton family was finally on the porch, and there—daddy's blood still high and hot from watching the old man's expert use of his stick—was my mother standing pink and in full flower under her thin cotton housedress. In that moment, any number of lives took new and irreversible direction.

Once he saw her, he didn't waste any time. Four months later, in November, they were married. She was sixteen, he twenty-three. Immediately there took place in him a change that has been taking place in men ever since they got out of their caves. As soon as he got himself a wife, he took off that white linen suit and put on a pair of overalls. He got out of that Model T Ford and put it up on blocks under Uncle Major's cotton shed because he didn't have enough money to drive it. He drove a mule and wagon instead. And he went to work with a vengeance. More than one person has told me that it wasn't his heart that killed him, that he simply worked himself to death.

Still, he must have cut a fine figure that blustery, freezing day in November of 1928, when he took my mother down to Ten Mile Missionary Baptist Church and married her in a small service attended only by blood kin. They were joined together by Preacher Will Davis, who two years earlier had baptized my mother in Ten Mile Creek, which is just down behind Ten Mile Missionary Baptist Church. They went to the church that day in a mule and wagon, as did most of the other people who came, and after they were married, they spent their wedding night at Uncle Major Eason's house. Uncle Major would one day own the livestock barn in Alma and become known as one of the best mule traders in Georgia. Uncle Major's first wife had died early and he was then married to my mama's sister Olive.

After spending the night under Uncle Major's tin roof in a deep feather bed, with the ground frozen outside, they got up the next morning and, still in a mule and wagon, went to the first farm they were to live on. Daddy had gone from being a young dandy in a white suit driving a Model T Ford to a married man in overalls sharecropping for a man named Luther Carter. They farmed the place on shares, which meant Luther Carter furnished the seed and the mules and the fertilizer for them to make the crop and at the end of the year they kept half of what they made.

In that little sharecropper's house of Luther Carter's they lived with Uncle John Carter and Aunt Ora, who was daddy's sister. Uncle John Carter was no kin to Luther Carter, but they were in Cartertown, where most people had that last name. The house had a wooden roof that leaked badly, no screens and wooden windows. There were two ten-by-ten bedrooms and a shotgun hall that ran the length of the house to the kitchen. They put up a partition in the middle of the kitchen, and Uncle John and Aunt Ora had one room to live in and the use of half the partitioned kitchen. Daddy and mama had the same arrangement on their side. Mama had a Home Comfort, Number 8, wood stove to cook on. There was a hot-water reservoir and four eyes on the cast-iron top of the stove, but it was a tiny thing, hardly more than three feet wide and two feet deep.

They brought to the house as wedding presents: a frying pan, an iron wash pot, four plates and as many knives and forks and spoons, an iron bedstead complete with slats and mattress, four quilts, four sheets, and a pillow. Daddy built everything else: a little cook table, a slightly larger table to eat off of, with a bench on each side instead of chairs, a chest of drawers, and an ironing board made from a plank wrapped in striped bed ticking. It was almost a year before they got two flatirons, one of which would be heated on the hearthstone while the other was being used.

The farm had sixty acres in cultivation, and so Luther Carter furnished Uncle John and daddy each a mule. Thirty acres was as much as one man and one mule could tend, and even then they had to step smart from first sun to last to do it. They had no cows or hogs and no smokehouse, and that first year they lived—as we did for much of my childhood—on fatback, grits, tea without ice, and biscuits made from flour and water and lard.

It was on the Luther Carter place that mama—with a midwife in attendance—lost her first child in the middle of August 1929, the year following their marriage. The baby was not born dead, but nearly so, its liver on the outside of its body. Its life lasted only a matter of minutes and mama didn't look at it but once before it was washed and dressed in a cotton gown and put in a coffin not much bigger than a breadbox and hauled in a wagon to Ten Mile Missionary Baptist Church, where it was buried in an unmarked grave. I don't know how wide the practice was or how it originated, but if a child was lost in miscarriage or born dead, or died nearly immediately from some gross deformity, there was never a marker put at its head.

I've tried to imagine what my daddy's thoughts must have been when the child was lost. He had told mama what happened down in the Everglades and in the town of Arcadia, and I know the death of his firstborn son must have hurt him profoundly. It was commonly believed then in Bacon County, and to some extent still is, that a miscarriage or a baby born dead or deformed was the consequence of some taint in the blood or taint in the moral life of the parents. I know daddy must have keenly felt all over again the crippled pleasure of that night so many months before under the palm-thatched chickee with the Seminole girl.

Maybe such thoughts are what drove him to work so hard. The sun always rose on him in the field, and he was still in the field when it set. He worked harder than the mule he plowed, did everything a man could do to bring something out of the sorry soil he worked, but that first year the crop failed. What this meant was that in August at the end of the crop year, he got half of nothing. They stayed alive on what they could borrow against the coming crop and what little help they could find from their people, who had not done well that year either.

Nearly everybody in the county had done worse that year than any of them could remember in a long time. Part of the reason, and probably the most important, was tobacco. Tobacco had come into the county as a money crop not many years before, and though eventually it turned into a blessing of sorts, for a long time it brought a series of economic disasters. It was a delicate crop, much dependent upon the weather. Most of the farmers were not yet skilled enough in all that was necessary to bring in a good crop: sowing the seeds in beds, transplanting from the beds to the field at the right time, proper amounts of fertilizer (too much would burn it up), suckering it, worming it, cropping it, stringing it, and cooking it in barns so that it turned out golden and valuable instead of dark and worthless.

Before tobacco came into Bacon County, the farmers were

self-sufficient in a way they were never to be again. In the days before tobacco they grew everything they needed and lived pretty well. Since they were too far south to grow wheat, they had to buy flour. But almost everything else they really wanted, they could grow. Grandpa Hazelton even grew rice on a piece of his low-lying land that had enough water to sustain that crop.

But tobacco took so much of their time and energy and worry that they stopped growing many of the crops they had grown before. Consequently, they had to depend upon the money from the tobacco to buy what they did not grow. A failed tobacco crop then was a genuine disaster that affected not just the individual farmer but the economy of the entire county.

Even if the tobacco crop was successful, all it meant, with rare exceptions, was for one brief moment at the end of summer they had money in their hands before they had to give it over to whoever supplied the fertilizer to grow the tobacco and the poison to kill the worms, and to those who helped harvest and cook it, and a hundred other expenses that ate up the money and put them right back in debt again. Tobacco money was then and is now an illusion, and growing tobacco became very quickly an almost magical rite they kept participating in over and over again, hoping that they would have a particularly good crop one year and they would be able to keep some of the money and not have to give it all away.

But the tobacco crop was not successful that first year on Luther Carter's place or anywhere else in the county, and daddy, along with everybody else, was desperate for money. On top of money worries, there was great pressure from Grandpa and Grandma Hazelton for daddy and mama to move back to the home place and live with them. Daddy didn't want to do it out of simple pride. Even though he was already a sharecropper, he didn't want to move in with and work for his wife's parents. He had never gotten along very well with Grandpa Hazelton, a man who liked to give much advice and do little work.

Grandpa spent most of his time reading the three newspapers

he subscribed to, newspapers brought by the mailman. It didn't bother him that the newspapers were always two or three days out of date; he read them all from the first page to the last, staying up until the small hours of the morning with a kerosene lamp beside him, all the while taking little sips out of a mason fruit jar full of moonshine which he kept on the mantelpiece over the fireplace. He didn't get drunk; he just liked to have little sips while he was awake.

He stopped only long enough to look about now and then to see if anybody was about to do something. If they were, he would explain in great and careful detail just how they should do it. He would do this whether he knew anything about the task at hand or not. Then he would go back to his newspaper.

Daddy was too proud and stubborn and independent for such an arrangement to work. But his wife was the youngest child of the family, still only seventeen years old. She had just lost a baby and the crops had failed, and so, against his better judgment, he went to live with his in-laws.

It was a total and unrelieved disaster that came to the point of crisis, strangely enough, over biscuits one night when they were all sitting at the supper table. Daddy looked up and saw Grandpa Hazelton smiling down the table at him.

Daddy said: "Something the matter?"

Since the old man was bad to bristle and bark himself, he said: "Is it look to be something the matter?"

"What you laughing at?"

"I ain't laughing."

"I seen it."

The old man said: "A man cain't tell me in my own house I was laughing."

Daddy said: "You was. And it was because of them biscuits."

"I don't laugh at biscuits, boy. I ain't crazy yet, even if it's some that think I am."

"You was laughing at how many I et. Was you counting, too?"

Daddy didn't have a very thick skin, and one of the things he was touchy about was how much he ate. Just a little over a

month before his run-in with the old man, he was at a church
picnic and Frank Porter, a boy from Coffee County, said something about him being Long Hungry, which to the people in
that time was an insult. To be Long Hungry meant you were a
glutton. A hog at the trough. So Daddy invited Frank Porter—
since they were at a church and couldn't settle it there—to
meet him the next day on a scrub oak ridge separating Coffee
from Bacon.

The next morning at sunup the two men met, daddy and the
man who had insulted him, up in the middle of a little stand of
blackjack oak on a sandy ridge full of gopher holes and rattle-
snake nests. They had each of them brought several of their
friends as overseers of the fight, or rather their friends had insisted on coming to make sure that no knives or axes or guns
got in the way and resulted in one or both of their deaths.

They set to and fought until noon, quit, went home, ate,
patched up as best they could, and came back and fought until
sundown. They didn't fight the whole time. By mutual consent
and necessity, they took time out to rest. While they were resting, their friends fought. Those that were there said it had
been a real fine day. A little bloody, but a fine day. For years
after the fight, time was often measured by farmers in both
counties by the day the fight took place.

*"It weren't no more'n two months after Ray and Frank met
up on the line."*

*"That girl of mine was born three months to the day before
Frank and Ray had the fight."*

And sitting there now at the supper table still smarting from
being called Long Hungry and still carrying sign on his back
and chest and head from the fight with Frank Porter, he could
not bear what he knew he saw in grandpa's face.

He stood up from the table and said to mama: "Myrtice, git
your things. We leavin."

Grandpa said: "Where you going to?"

Daddy stopped just long enough to say, "I don't know where
I'm going. It's lots of places I could go. What you don't understand, old man, is if I didn't have anyplace to go, I'd go
anyway."

But he had a place to go and he knew it. Uncle Alton had recently been married to a lady named Eva Jenkins and they were sharecropping themselves for Jess Boatwright. Summer was coming on and all the crops had been laid by, which meant they'd been plowed the last time and all that remained was the harvest. Daddy put mama on the wagon seat beside him and started the long slow ride over the dirt roads in the dark to offer Uncle Alton a proposition which in his heart he didn't believe Uncle Alton would take. Since he was sharecropping for grandpa, he meant to trade crops.

"We got to swap," he said when Uncle Alton came to the door.

"Swap what?" Uncle Alton said.

"You take my crop and I'll take yours. You and Eva go and live with your daddy, cause I cain't stand it. Me and Myrtice'll come live here."

Daddy told him what had happened, and Uncle Alton never questioned it, knowing as he did how his daddy was. Also, daddy was his best friend and mama his baby sister. He knew daddy would never consent to going back after leaving in the middle of the night that way. They had to live somewhere. There were no options.

"We'll swap even," Uncle Alton said.

"I ought to give you something to boot," daddy said. "You got ten acres more'n me."

Uncle Alton said: "We'll swap even."

And they did. It made quite a noise in the county. Nobody had ever heard of such a thing. Some of the old folks still talk to this day about that trade, about how daddy and mama moved into the house on the Jess Boatwright place and Uncle Alton and Aunt Eva went over to live with Grandpa Hazelton.

Daddy never set foot in grandpa's house again as long as he lived. He would allow mama to go and visit and after my brother and I were born to take us with her.

After they finished gathering the crop, which was good enough to let them get far enough out of debt to borrow on the next crop, they rented the Jess Boatwright place for one year. But as the world seems to go sometimes when a man's got his back right up against the wall, the tobacco crop that year was so sorry daddy couldn't even sell it, and he ended by putting it in the mule stable instead.

Cotton that year was selling for three cents a pound and you could buy a quarter of beef for four cents a pound. It was 1931. The rest of the country was just beginning to feel the real hurt of the Great Depression, but it had been living in Bacon County for years. Some folks said it had always been there.

But in that year two good things did happen. On the ninth of July, mama gave birth to a healthy baby, who was named after daddy, Ray, but who has always been called Hoyet. The other thing that happened was that daddy somehow managed to buy a mare. A mare, not a mule. Her name was Daisy, and she was so mean that daddy was the only one in the county who could put a bridle on her, much less work her to a plow or wagon. It was the first draft animal he'd owned, and he was almost as proud of the mare as he was of his son.

As mean as she was, Daisy pulled a fine wagon and even a better plow if you could control her. As it turned out, daddy could control her. He had her respect and she had his. They knew what to expect from one another. He knew dead solid certain that she would kick his head off if she got the chance. And she knew just as surely that he would beat her to her knees with a singletree—the iron bar on a plow or wagon to which the trace chains are hooked—if she did not cooperate.

It sounds like a terrible thing to talk about, hitting a mare between the ears with a piece of iron, but it was done not only out of necessity but also out of love. A farmer didn't mistreat his draft animals. People in Bacon County always said that a man who would mistreat his mules would mistreat his family. But it was necessary for daddy and Daisy to come to some understanding before they could do the work that was proper to both of them. And whatever was necessary to that understanding had to be done. Without that understanding, there could be no respect, to say nothing of love. For a man and an animal to work together from sunup to dark, day in and day out, there ought to be love. How else could either of them bear it?

Still, it was unusual for him to have a mare instead of a mule. Horses and mares were playthings. Mules were the workers. Mules bought the baby's shoes and put grits on the table.

I never remember seeing anybody plow a horse in Bacon County, and it wasn't because mules were cheaper than horses. They weren't. Daddy got Daisy for $60. A good young mule even in the depth of the Depression would have cost him $200. So it was not because of cost that farmers plowed mules instead of horses; it was because horses have no stamina in front of a turnplow breaking dirt a foot deep. Worse, a horse doesn't care where he puts his feet. A mule puts his foot down exactly where he means to put it. A mule will walk all day, straight as a plumb line, setting his feet down only inches from young corn, corn that might be less than a foot high, and he'll never step on a plant. A horse walks all over everything. Unless, that is, you can come to some understanding with him, which most men did not seem to be able to do. But daddy made a sweet working animal out of Daisy, and she was ready, if not always willing, to do whatever was required of her. In the shoebox of pictures, there is one of my brother when he was only four years old sitting on Daisy bareback. Nobody is holding her rein and she is standing easy as the lady she became under my daddy's firm, gentle, and dangerous hand.

Maybe it was because of the crops failing or the trouble they'd had with Grandpa Hazelton, but mama remembers the house at the Jess Boatwright place as the worst they ever lived in. It was made out of notched logs, but instead of being mud-sealed, it was board-sealed, which meant the wind had a free way with it in the winter. My brother had a case of double pneumonia that year and almost died. There was no smoke-house, so the little bit of meat they could come by was cured by hanging in the sun during the day and then putting it in the shed at night. They also put some of it in stone jugs of brine to preserve it, but while meat never spoiled in a jug of brine, it took real courage and a certain desperation to eat through all that salt.

But luck fortunately comes in two flavors: good as well as

bad. And some good luck came their way at the end of the second year on the Jess Boatwright place. My Grandma Hazelton gave them 120 acres of land. What wealth there was in the Hazelton family at that time came through my grandma. Grandpa Hazelton brought very little to the marriage and what little he brought got away from him somehow while he read his three newspapers every day. But Grandma Hazelton's daddy left her a big piece of land and they—she and grandpa—built the house they lived in out of the sale of part of it. But there was a good bit left, and because mama was the youngest in the family, and because of the tragic circumstances of her firstborn child, and maybe also to try somehow to make up for daddy and mama having to trade crops with Uncle Alton and move out of the house in the middle of the year, she made the land a gift outright, and they went to live on it.

But even good luck rarely comes made out of whole cloth, and theirs had several pretty ragged places in it. For starters, none of the land was in cultivation. It was nothing but pine trees and palmetto thickets and stands of gallberry bushes and dog fennel. Worse than that, if there can be anything worse than a farmer with no land he can farm, there was no house on it, no building of any kind. There was nothing for daddy to do but build one.

And he did. Uncle Randal Jordan and one of my daddy's good friends, Cadger Barnes, helped him. Daddy paid them a wage of a quarter a day. None of the trees on the land they'd been given were big enough to use, so Cadger, who had a heavy stand of big pine on his land, gave daddy enough trees to build the house. And the three of them, using crosscut saws, felled the trees and snaked the logs over to the place with Daisy, and then they cut the trees into lengths they could split for boards. There was no money for a sawmill, so with wedges and mallets and axes they split the pine by hand into boards.

Once it was finished you could smell the turpentine out of that green pine house from a mile away. The whole house cost $50 to build. Mama planted a cedar tree out in the front yard the day they moved in. It was the house in which I would be born. The house is gone now, but I stood in the shade of that cedar tree four months ago.

The first year they were there daddy cleared ten acres for cultivation. The second year he cleared another ten. He and mama did it together with an ax and a saw and a grubbing hoe and Daisy. Daisy pulled what she could from the ground. What she couldn't pull out, mama and daddy dug out. What they couldn't dig out, they burned out. There were a few people, very few, who could afford dynamite to blow stumps out; everybody else dug and burned, burned and dug. An oak stump might cost a man a week of his life.

All through the winter of that second year, the hazy smoke of burning stumps floated over them as they picked up roots and grubbed palmetto and gallberry. Mama had been growing pinker and rounder and seemingly stronger every day with her third and what would prove to be her last pregnancy. She didn't quit going to the field until May, and on the seventh of June, 1935, Daddy got on Daisy and went over to get Emily Ahl, who came racing back behind his galloping mare in her midwifery buggy in which she had gone to farmhouses all over that end of Bacon County.

In the late afternoon, Miss Emily, wearing her black bonnet and black, long dress, a dress and color she considered proper to her calling, cut me loose from mama and tied me off. She was a midwife of consummate skill, and my entrance into the world was without incident.

I am compelled to celebrate the craft and art of the lady who did everything that was required of her so competently. Not only did she make a lovely arrangement of my navel when she cut me free, but she also left me intact, for which I have always been grateful.

Since they had no land to tend while they were taking in the new ground, daddy rented thirty acres from the land bank, a federal agency that controlled a lot of land and let it to farmers at a cost they could afford, which meant practically nothing. In his spare time, when he wasn't farming the acreage he'd rented from the land bank or pulling stumps or working on the stable for Daisy, he hired out to plow for other people. Mama would pack him some biscuit and fatback and maybe a vegetable she might have put up the previous summer, along with a little cold grits; she'd put it all in a tin syrup bucket, and he'd leave the house before sunup and come back after dark, bringing the empty syrup bucket and twenty-five cents for his day's work.

By the time I was born he'd put up a mule barn and a notched log smokehouse sealed with mud. Just when he got the place looking pretty good, he had the chance to sell it at more than he'd thought he'd ever be able to make out of it again, and at the same time the chance to buy a place cheap that he'd been looking at a long time. So he sold out and bought the Cash Carter place, which had a little better than 200 acres of land— about 40 of it in cultivation. He got it at a good price because the land had been allowed to lie fallow until it was rank with weeds. Most of the fences were down, there was no mule lot or smokehouse or tobacco barn, and the dwelling house was nearly as sorry as the one they'd lived in at Jess Boatwright's. But it was 200 acres of land, and daddy knew, or thought he knew, that he could make it into a decent farm on which he could support his family. It wouldn't be easy and it wouldn't be quick, but given five or ten years, he would do it and he would do it right.

CHAPTER 3

In early December 1935 daddy loaded us up in the wagon with Daisy between the shaves. He put the mattress and bedsteads and table and benches and the Home Comfort, Number 8, stove—put it all in the wagon with me, six months old at the time, and my brother, who was four years old, up on the mattress bundled in quilts, and mama beside him on the crossboard and started down the six miles of washboard road to the Cash Carter place.

Cash Carter didn't own it; it just went by his name. If the house were still standing today, it would still go by his name. A farm in Bacon County took a man's name, not always the first man who owned it, but some man's name, and once the name was taken, it held the name as long as it stood, no matter who lived there. It was a tradition that gave direction to the county. Farmers as a rule didn't move around much, but subsistence farmers—tenants out on the fringe of things—moved a lot, much more than most people would imagine, moved from one patch of farmed-out land to another, from one failed crop to a place where they thought there was hope of making a good one. Because they moved, it helped for the farms to hold the same name forever. It gave people's lives points of reference.

When we got there, daddy had to start building all over again. He worked from very early in the morning until very late at night, usually for as long as he and Daisy could see. During that first year he built a log tobacco barn and a lot for Daisy, and in the fall of the following year he managed to put up a little tenant house himself and move widow Ella Thomas into it with her three boys, ages ten, fourteen, and sixteen. They worked with daddy and mama, hoeing and weeding the forty acres in cultivation, helping with the turpentine timber, and taking in new ground. He paid the family fifty cents a day in wages.

It pleases me that right after daddy moved to the Cash Carter place he became good friends with the sorriest man in the county, Pete Fretch. Pete's affectionate name for his wife was "nigger." She was a thin, starved gray thing who moved about quiet as a shadow on her bare feet. Her mouth, nearly toothless, was always stained by the cud of snuff caught between lip and gum. Pete, when he wasn't busy telling lies or stealing, used to spend his time whipping his wife with a four-plait cowwhip.

Anybody in that part of the county who had something stolen would just go on over to Pete's little tar-paper shack and say: "All right, Pete, where's my wheelbarrow?" or "Where's my singletrees?" or "Where's my shoat hog?" And Pete, if he had whatever was missing, and he usually did, would give it up, always with a marvelous and convoluted excuse about how the hog had just wandered up to his place, or how he'd been walking down by the Harrikin four days ago to go catfishing and happened to find the singletrees in a ditch. He'd say he wondered at the time who them singletrees belonged to and how come they were in the ditch.

But if the notion struck him, and it almost never did, Pete could do just about anything there was to do. He could build a good drawing chimney, a chimney that would never back up and smoke the house, or he could butcher a hog quicker than a blink (no doubt from long practice of butchering other people's hogs in the woods and making off with the meat before he was caught) or make the best sausage meat in South Georgia or build anything: houses or barns or lots, the boards of which were true as a plumb line and tight as if they'd been made of brick.

In 1936, he built a wash trough for mama. She washed clothes in that trough for as long as we farmed. It was made out of a tree three feet thick and twenty feet long. He dug out one end of it for a place where mama could wash her clothes and dug out the other end for a place to rinse. He made it using a chisel and an ax and a drawing knife and fire. He chopped and hewed and chipped and burned it deeper, smoothed it out with litered knots. Finally, he flattened off the bottom so it would stand steady. When he finished, it was so symmetrical it might have been calibrated on a machine.

Daddy tried to give him a quarter for his work. Pete refused it. This strange, sorry, violent man would not spend one minute of his life doing anything for anybody for cash money. But he would do anything for a friend and *always* refuse money for it. Since there was hardly anybody who could stand him as a friend, the question of whether or not to work rarely came up.

Daddy had worked progressively harder since the day he got married. He was having a lot of trouble with his heart, and it wasn't unusual for him to fall in the field. He might fall anywhere, doing anything, and sometimes it was as much as an hour before he could move about freely again. But as soon as he could, he went directly back to the task at hand. He had also lost the two front teeth out of his top gum from pyorrhea, and his weight was down to 155 pounds. He had, as they said, gone to nothing but breath and britches. But he insisted on working as hard as ever. It was his custom to get up in the morning and build a fire in the stove, leaving mama and my brother and me in the bed asleep and get out to the lot, bridle and harness Daisy, and get to the field and work there until mama took a hammer and beat on an old plow point hanging up on the front porch.

When he heard the ringing plow point, he would come to the house, eat his breakfast, and go directly back to the field. The same thing was repeated at dinnertime in the middle of the day and again at night. It was an unusual day when he didn't go back to the field if it was light enough to see after he had eaten supper. If it was too dark to go back to the field, he worked on the mule lot or on the tenant house or on Daisy's harness, which he managed to hold together with baling wire.

His color had gone bad. There was a wildness in his eyes,

but he resisted going to the doctor. Doctors meant money, and the little he had he desperately needed to keep everything together: the farm, his wife and babies.

It was during this time when daddy was working himself to death, practically living in the field, that something happened that will forever epitomize the experience of my people. It was a bright, hot summer day. It had not rained in nearly a month. The crop was doing well that year. Mama had been cleaning house since daylight and was scrubbing the floor of the last room, using homemade lye and a scrub brush made out of cornshucks.

It was midafternoon, and as she worked, she could see daddy through the open, screenless window out in the field. He was spraying the tobacco for cutworms. While she scrubbed, I was in the doorway leading into the room in a little playpen daddy had built for me.

They had done better than usual the first year there on the Cash Carter place and had managed to buy two yearling cows, the first they had ever owned. She looked up from her work and saw the two yearlings walking along the fence row toward the barrel of lead poisoning daddy had in a turpentine barrel on a sled. Mama knew they were going to drink out of the barrel, and if they did, they would die right where they were standing because the poison daddy was putting on the tobacco was deadly.

She leaned out of the window and hollered for him, but he was down between the tobacco rows with the sprayer, a long metal cylinder that was filled with air pressure using a hand pump. The sprayer was strapped to his back, and the hissing air and blowing spray made it impossible for him to hear her. So she threw down her shuck scrub brush and ran out of the house toward the field.

Halfway there, she heard me scream and knew immediately what had happened. When she got back to the house, I had turned over my playpen and crawled into the room where she had been working. Some of the pieces of lye had not melted, and I was sitting on the floor screaming, holding a lump of raw lye in each hand, and worse, I had put some of it in my mouth. Blood was running from my lips and tongue. She snatched me up and ran for daddy, who put Daisy to the wagon, and they galloped the eight miles to town to Dr. Sharp's office.

It turned out not to be as bad as it looked. I had not swallowed any of the lye, and the burns in my mouth and on my hands were not serious.

When they got back home, the yearling cows were dead, lying already stiff by the barrel of lead poisoning.

Daddy strapped the sprayer on and went back to work in the tobacco. He worked until it was so dark he couldn't see, and then he hitched Daisy to the only two cows he'd ever owned and dragged them off behind the field for the buzzards to eat. He was afraid to butcher them because of the poison.

Ever since mama first told me that story of the day they lost the cows I have thought a great deal about my daddy in that time, of how tragic it was and how typical. The world that circumscribed the people I come from had so little margin for error, for bad luck, that when something went wrong, it almost always brought something else down with it. It was a world in which survival depended on raw courage, a courage born out of desperation and sustained by a lack of alternatives.

When the crop was finally gathered and sold, daddy took most of the money he had made that year, sold the turpentine rights to his timber, and paid off the mortgage that the bank held on the place. In spite of all that had happened, things were looking pretty good for him. He owned a little over 200 acres free and clear, and he had enough money to start his next crop.

But that same year on April 17, 1937, it all caught up with him, and he went down. They had a particularly bad winter, and even in mid-April it was still cold. All of us were sleeping in the same bed that night. Mama woke up shortly after dawn and was surprised to see him still in the bed beside her. No fire in the stove, none in the fireplace. And daddy still in bed where the light of day never found him. But he had butchered hogs not long before that and prepared the smokehouse to cure the meat, all of which is exhausting work, and she thought he was just tired out from it all and had overslept. She got quietly out of bed, got a fire going in the stove, and made breakfast.

About the time she got the grits bubbling and the biscuits in the oven and the water heated in the reservoir and the kitchen warm from the stove, my brother, who was then five years old, came walking in, yawning, wearing his cotton gown. Mama told him to go in and wake up his daddy. He went back into the bedroom and stood beside the bed watching his daddy and watching me, then twenty-one months old, sleeping at his side. Hoyet thought to play a trick on his daddy, an affectionate little-boy trick, and he reached over and twisted his daddy's nose to wake him up, twisted it gently, and then harder, and finally harder still. But daddy didn't move.

He went back into the kitchen and said: "Daddy won't wake up and his nose is cold."

He was dead, had died sometime in the night in his sleep of a massive heart attack, so massive and so sudden that he didn't move enough to wake his wife, who was sleeping with her head on his arm.

She screamed and ran into the yard. She stood there for a long time mindlessly screaming in a terror for her husband's death. Her screaming brought widow Ella Thomas out of her little tenant house, and then her three children, and finally the house that day was filled with her people and daddy's.

The door was taken down, as it usually was in those days, for a cooling board, and the body placed upon it. Ordinarily the women of the family would have gathered and washed the corpse and dressed it and closed its eyes and combed its hair and shaved it for burial. But mama, for reasons she cannot now name, but which I have always thought of as a statement of her love and respect for her husband, had an embalmer come from Waycross, thirty miles away.

When daddy was drained of blood, the blood was buried out behind the house in a deep hole but not deep enough to keep a dog we had then, a hound dog whose name was Sam, from knowing what was buried there. Sam lay on the buried blood and howled all night and continued to howl for three

days and nights running until he was almost dead himself
from exhaustion because he would take no food or water.

Even the coffin was not built by the men of the family, as it
customarily would have been. Rather, it was brought from the
Mincy Funeral Home, the same place the embalmer came
from in Waycross. Daddy was dressed in the only suit of
clothes he had and placed in his box. The entire expense for
the coffin, having it brought from Waycross, and the job of
work done by the embalmer was just under $60.

Two days later, on April 19, 1937, the coffin was loaded
onto the wagon he bought with the money from the sale of the
Model T Ford that he'd put up on blocks all those years ago.
Daisy was hitched to the wagon, and other wagons drawn by
mules carrying members of the family set off for Corinth Free-
will Baptist Church ten miles away. One of the men riding the
second wagon with his wife, Dinah, was daddy's older brother
Pascal. Eight months later, in December, Pascal would be di-
vorced from Dinah and mama would marry him.

They went the long slow way to the graveyard there behind
a tiny white clapboard church and put daddy in the ground
with a wooden marker at his head. Later mama would find the
money, $150, for a slab and headstone of Georgia marble. The
same man who had baptized her when she was fourteen and
later joined her and daddy in marriage, Preacher Will Davis,
said the last words over the open grave on that day unlike
April at all, but rainy and blustery and still cold.

The two closest graves to the one daddy lies in today are the
graves of babies. One died in 1927 and the other in 1928. They
were both Smith babies. The first one had lived to be ten
months old, the other eight months old. For reasons I cannot
name, it has always seemed profoundly right to me that two
babies lie there so close to him who cared so much for babies
and who had been told so early that he would never have any
and who, once having them, lost them not because they died,
but because he himself went down so early.

The night after the day daddy was buried, somebody went
in the smokehouse and stole all the meat that had been cured
and hung there before he died. There were nine middlings of

meat hanging, and sausage in boxes, and headcheese in muslin cloth, and somebody took it all, everything but one little piece about as big as a man's hand hanging in the back of the smoke-house.

Mama knows who got the meat, not because she has any hard proof, but because in her heart she knows, and I know, too, but the one who got it is himself lying in the same grave-yard daddy's in and I see no reason to name him.

He was one of my daddy's friends. I do not say he was *sup-posedly* or *apparently* a friend. He *was* a friend, and a close one, but he stole the meat anyway. Not many people may be able to understand that or sympathize with it, but I think I do. It was a hard time in that land, and a lot of men did things for which they were ashamed and suffered for the rest of their lives. But they did them because of hunger and sickness and because they could not bear the sorry spectacle of their chil-dren dying from lack of a doctor and their wives growing old before they were thirty.

PART 2

PART 2

CHAPTER 4

It has always seemed to me that I was not so much born into this life as I awakened to it. I remember very distinctly the awakening and the morning it happened. It was my first glimpse of myself, and all that I know now—the stories, and everything conjured up by them, that I have been writing about thus far—I obviously knew none of then, particularly anything about my real daddy, whom I was not to hear of until I was nearly six years old, not his name, not even that he was my daddy. Or if I did hear of him, I have no memory of it.

I awoke in the middle of the morning in early summer from the place I'd been sleeping in the curving roots of a giant oak tree in front of a large white house. Off to the right, beyond the dirt road, my goats were trailing along in the ditch, grazing in the tough wire grass that grew there. Their constant bleating shook the warm summer air. I always thought of them as my goats although my brother usually took care of them. Before he went to the field that morning to work, he had let them out of the old tobacco barn where they slept at night. At my feet was a white dog whose name was Sam. I looked at the dog and at the house and at the red gown with little pearl-colored buttons I was wearing, and I knew that the gown had been made for me by my Grandma Hazelton and that the dog belonged to me. He went everywhere I went, and he always took precious care of me.

Precious. That was my mama's word for how it was between Sam and me, even though Sam caused her some inconvenience from time to time. If she wanted to whip me, she had to take me in the house, where Sam was never allowed to go. She could never touch me when I was crying if Sam could help it. He would move quietly—he was a dog not given to barking very much—between the two of us and show her his teeth. Unless she took me somewhere Sam couldn't go, there'd be no punishment for me.

The house there just behind me, partially under the arching limbs of the oak tree, was called the Williams place. It was where I lived with my mama and my brother, Hoyet, and my daddy, whose name was Pascal. I knew when I opened my eyes that morning that the house was empty because everybody had gone to the field to work. I also knew, even though I couldn't remember doing it, that I had awakened sometime in midmorning and come out onto the porch and down the steps and across the clean-swept dirt yard through the gate weighted with broken plow points so it would swing shut behind me, that I had come out under the oak tree and lain down against the curving roots with my dog, Sam, and gone to sleep. It was a thing I had done before. If I ever woke up and the house was empty and the weather was warm—which was the only time I would ever awaken to an empty house—I always went out under the oak tree to finish my nap. It wasn't fear or loneliness that drove me outside; it was just something I did for reasons I would never be able to discover.

I stood up and stretched and looked down at my bare feet at the hem of the gown and said: "I'm almost five and already a great big boy." It was my way of reassuring myself, but it was also something my daddy said about me and it made me feel good because in his mouth it seemed to mean I was almost a man.

Sam immediately stood up too, stretched, reproducing, as he always did, every move I made, watching me carefully to see which way I might go. I knew I ought not to be outside lying in the rough curve of root in my cotton gown. Mama didn't mind me being out there under the tree, but I was supposed to get dressed first. Sometimes I did; often I forgot.

So I turned and went back through the gate, Sam at my heels, and across the yard and up the steps onto the porch to the front door. When I opened the door, Sam stopped and lay down to wait. He would be there when I came out, no matter which door I used. If I went out the back door, he would some-how magically know it and he would be there. If I came out the side door by the little pantry, he would know that, too, and he would be there. Sam always knew where I was, and he made it his business to be there, waiting.

I went into the long, dim, cool hallway that ran down the center of the house. Briefly I stopped at the bedroom where my parents slept and looked in at the neatly made bed and all the parts of the room, clean, with everything where it was sup-posed to be, just the way mama always kept it. And I thought of daddy, as I so often did because I loved him so much. If he was sitting down, I was usually in his lap. If he was standing up, I was usually holding his hand. He always said soft funny things to me and told me stories that never had an end but al-ways continued when we met again.

He was tall and lean with flat high cheekbones and deep eyes and black thick hair which he combed straight back on his head. And under the eye on his left cheek was the scarred print of a perfect set of teeth. I knew he had taken the scar in a fight, but I never asked him about it and the teeth marks in his cheek only made him seem more powerful and stronger and special to me.

He shaved every morning at the water shelf on the back porch with a straight razor and always smelled of soap and whiskey. I knew mama did not like the whiskey, but to me it smelled sweet, better even than the soap. And I could never understand why she resisted it so, complained of it so, and kept telling him over and over again that he would kill himself and ruin everything if he continued with the whiskey. I did not understand about killing himself and I did not understand about ruining everything, but I knew the whiskey somehow caused the shouting and screaming and the ugly sound of breaking things in the night. The stronger the smell of whiskey on him, though, the kinder and gentler he was with me and my brother.

I went on down the hallway and out onto the back porch and finally into the kitchen that was built at the very rear of the house. The entire room was dominated by a huge black cast-iron stove with six eyes on its cooking surface. Directly across the room from the stove was the safe, a tall square cabinet with wide doors covered with screen wire that was used to keep biscuits and fried meat and rice or almost any other kind of food that had been recently cooked. Between the stove and the safe sat the table we ate off of, a table almost ten feet long, with benches on each side instead of chairs, so that when we put in tobacco, there would be enough room for the hired hands to eat.

I opened the safe, took a biscuit off a plate, and punched a hole in it with my finger. Then with a jar of cane syrup, I poured the hole full, waited for it to soak in good, and then poured again. When the biscuit had all the syrup it would take, I got two pieces of fried pork off another plate and went out and sat on the back steps, where Sam was already lying in the warm sun, his ears struck forward on his head. I ate the bread and pork slowly, chewing for a long time and sharing it all with Sam.

When we had finished, I went back into the house, took off my gown, and put on a cotton undershirt, my overalls with twin galluses that buckled on my chest, and my straw hat, which was rimmed on the edges with a border of green cloth and had a piece of green cellophane sewn into the brim to act as an eyeshade. I was barefoot, but I wished very much I had a pair of brogans because brogans were what men wore and I very much wanted to be a man. In fact, I was pretty sure I already was a man, but the only one who seemed to know it was my daddy. Everybody else treated me like I was still a baby.

I went out the side door, and Sam fell into step behind me as we walked out beyond the mule barn where four mules stood in the lot and on past the cotton house and then down the dim road past a little leaning shack where our tenant farmers lived, a black family in which there was a boy just a year older than I was. His name was Willalee Bookatee. I went on past their house because I knew they would be in the field, too, so there was no use to stop.

I went through a sapling thicket and over a shallow ditch and finally climbed a wire fence into the field, being very careful of my overalls on the barbed wire. I could see them all, my family and the black tenant family, far off there in the shimmering heat of the tobacco field. They were pulling cutworms off the tobacco. I wished I could have been out there with them pulling worms because when you found one, you had to break it in half, which seemed great good fun to me. But you could also carry an empty Prince Albert tobacco can in your back pocket and fill it up with worms to play with later.

Mama wouldn't let me pull worms because she said I was too little and might damage the plants. If I was alone in the field with daddy, though, he would let me hunt all the worms I wanted to. He let me do pretty much anything I wanted to, which included sitting in his lap to guide his old pickup truck down dirt roads all over the county.

I went down to the end of the row and sat under a persimmon tree in the shade with Sam and watched as daddy and mama and brother and Willalee Bookatee, who was—I could see even from this distance—puting worms in Prince Albert cans, and his mama, whose name was Katie, and his daddy, whose name was Will, I watched them all as they came toward me, turning the leaves and searching for worms as they came.

The moment I sat down in the shade, I was already wondering how long it would be before they quit to go to the house for dinner because I was already beginning to wish I'd taken two biscuits instead of one and maybe another piece of meat, or else that I hadn't shared with Sam.

Bored, I looked down at Sam and said: "Sam, if you don't quit eatin my biscuit and meat, I'm gone have to cut you like a shoat hog."

A black cloud of gnats swarmed around his heavy muzzle, but I clearly heard him say that he didn't think I was man enough to do it. Sam and I talked a lot together, had long involved conversations, mostly about which one of us had done the other one wrong and, if not about that, about which one of us was the better man. It would be a good long time before I

started thinking of Sam as a dog instead of a person, But I always came out on top when we talked because Sam could only
say what I said he said, think what I thought he thought.

"If you was any kind of man atall, you wouldn't snap at
them gnats and eat them flies the way you do," I said.

"It ain't a thing in the world the matter with eatin gnats and
flies," he said.

"It's how come people treat you like a dog," I said. "You
could probably come on in the house like other folks if it
weren't for eatin flies and gnats like you do."

That's the way the talk went until daddy and the rest of
them finally came down to where Sam and I were sitting in the
shade. They stopped beside us to wipe their faces and necks
with sweat rags. Mama asked if I had got something to eat
when I woke up. I told her I had.

"You all gone stop for dinner now?"

"I reckon we'll work awhile longer," daddy said.

I said: "Well then, can Willalee and me go up to his house
and play till dinnertime?"

Daddy looked at the sun to see what time it was. He could
come within five or ten minutes by the position of the sun.
Most of the farmers I knew could.

Daddy was standing almost dead center in his own shadow.
"I reckon so," he said.

Then the whole thing had to be done over again. Willalee
asked his daddy the same question. Because my daddy had
said it was all right didn't mean Willalee's daddy would agree.
He usually did, but not always. So it was necessary to ask.

We climbed the fence and went across the ditch and back
through the sapling thicket to the three-track road that led up to
the shack, and while we walked, Willalee showed me the two
Prince Albert tobacco cans he had in his back pockets. They
were both filled with cutworms. The worms had lots of legs and
two little things on their heads that looked like horns. They
were about an inch long, sometimes as long as two inches, and
round and fat and made wonderful things to play with. There
was no fence around the yard where Willalee lived and the
whole house leaned toward the north at about a ten-degree

tilt. Before we even got up the steps, we could smell the food already cooking on the wood stove at the back of the house where his grandma was banging metal pots around over the cast-iron stove. Her name was Annie, but everybody called her Auntie. She was too old to work in the field anymore, but she was handy about the house with ironing and cooking and scrubbing floors and canning vegetables out of the field and berries out of the woods.

She also was full of stories, which, when she had the time—and she usually did—she told to me and Willalee and his little sister, whose name was Lottie Mae. Willalee and my brother and I called her Snottie Mae, but she didn't seem to mind. She came out of the front door when she heard us coming up on the porch and right away wanted to know if she could play in the book with us. She was the same age as I and sometimes we let her play with us, but most of the time we did not.

"Naw," Willalee said, "git on back in there and help Auntie. We ain't studying you."

"Bring us the book," I said.

"I git it for you," she said, "if you give me five of them worms."

"I ain't studying you," said Willalee.

She had already seen the two Prince Albert cans full of green worms because Willalee was sitting on the floor now, the lids of the cans open and the worms crawling out. He was lining two of them up for a race from one crack in the floor to the next crack, and he was arranging the rest of the worms in little designs of diamonds and triangles in some game he had not yet discovered the rules for.

"You bring the book," I said, "and you can have two of them worms."

Willalee almost never argued with what I decided to do, up to and including giving away the worms he had spent all morning collecting in the fierce summer heat, which is probably why I liked him so much. Lottie Mae went back into the house, and got the Sears, Roebuck catalogue and brought it out onto the porch. He handed her the two worms and told her to go on back in the house, told her it weren't fitting for her to be out here playing with worms while Auntie was back in the kitchen working.

"Ain't nothing left for me to do but put them plates on the table," she said.

"See to them plates then," Willalee said. As young as she was, Lottie Mae had things to do about the place. Whatever she could manage. We all did.

Willalee and I stayed there on the floor with the Sears, Roebuck catalogue and the open Prince Albert cans, out of which deliciously fat worms crawled. Then we opened the catalogue at random as we always did, to see what magic was waiting for us there.

In the minds of most people, the Sears, Roebuck catalogue is a kind of low joke associated with outhouses. God knows the catalogue sometimes ended up in the outhouse, but more often it did not. All the farmers, black and white, kept dried corncobs beside their double-seated thrones, and the cobs served the purpose for which they were put there with all possible efficiency and comfort.

The Sears, Roebuck catalogue was much better used as a Wish Book, which it was called by the people out in the country, who would never be able to order anything out of it, but could at their leisure spend hours dreaming over.

Willalee Bookatee and I used it for another reason. We made up stories out of it, used it to spin a web of fantasy about us. Without that catalogue our childhood would have been radically different. The federal government ought to strike a medal for the Sears, Roebuck company for sending all those catalogues to farming families, for bringing all that color and all that mystery and all that beauty into the lives of country people.

I first became fascinated with the Sears catalogue because all the people in its pages were perfect. Nearly everybody I knew had something missing, a finger cut off, a toe split, an ear half-chewed away, an eye clouded with blindness from a glancing fence staple. And if they didn't have something missing, they were carrying scars from barbed wire, or knives, or fishhooks. But the people in the catalogue had no such hurts. They were not only whole, had all their arms and legs and toes and eyes on their unscarred bodies, but they were also beautiful. Their legs were straight and their heads were never bald and on their faces were looks of happiness, even joy, looks that I never saw much of in the faces of the people around me.

Young as I was, though, I had known for a long time that it was all a lie. I knew that under those fancy clothes there had to be scars, there had to be swellings and boils of one kind or another because there was no other way to live in the world. And more than that, at some previous, unremembered moment, I had decided that all the people in the catalogue were related, not necessarily blood kin, but knew one another, and because they knew one another there had to be hard feelings, trouble between them off and on, violence, and hate between them as well as love. And it was out of this knowledge that I first began to make up stories about the people I found in the book.

Once I began to make up stories about them, Willalee and Lottie Mae began to make up stories, too. The stories they made up were every bit as good as mine. Sometimes better. More than once we had spent whole rainy afternoons when it was too wet to go to the field turning the pages of the catalogue, forcing the beautiful people to give up the secrets of their lives: how they felt about one another, what kind of sicknesses they may have had, what kind of scars they carried in their flesh under all those bright and fancy clothes.

Willalee had his pocketknife out and was about to operate on one of the green cutworms because he liked to pretend he was a doctor. It was I who first put the notion in his head that he might in fact be a doctor, and since we almost never saw a doctor and because they were mysterious and always drove cars or else fine buggies behind high-stepping mares, quickly healing people with their secret medicines, the notion stuck in Willalee's head, and he became very good at taking cutworms and other things apart with his pocketknife.

The Sears catalogue that we had opened at random found a

man in his middle years but still strong and healthy with a head full of hair and clear, direct eyes looking out at us, dressed in a red hunting jacket and wading boots, with a rack of shotguns behind him. We used our fingers to mark the spot and turned the Wish Book again, and this time it opened to ladies standing in their underwear, lovely as none we had ever seen, all perfect in their unstained clothes. Every last one of them had the same direct and steady eyes of the man in the red hunting jacket.

I said: "What do you think, Willalee?"

Without hesitation, Willalee said: "This lady here in her step-ins is his chile."

We kept the spot marked with the lady in the step-ins and the man in the hunting jacket and turned the book again, and there was a young man in a suit, the creases sharp enough to shave with, posed with his foot casually propped on a box, every strand of his beautiful hair in place.

"See, what it is," I said. "This boy right here is seeing that girl back there, the one in her step-ins, and she is the youngun of him back there, and them shotguns behind'm belong to him, and he ain't happy."

"Why he ain't happy?"

"Cause this feller standing here in this suit looking so nice, he ain't nice at all. He's mean, but he don't look mean. That gal is the only youngun the feller in the jacket's got, and he loves her cause she is a sweet child. He don't want her fooling with that sorry man in that suit. He's so sorry he done got his-self in trouble with the law. The high sheriff is looking for him right now. Him in the suit will fool around on you."

"How it is he fool around?"

"He'll steal anything he can put his hand to," I said. "He'll steal your hog, or he'll steal your cow out of your field. He's so sorry he'll take that cow if it's the only cow you got. It's just the kind of feller he is."

Willalee said: "Then how come it is she mess around with him?"

"That suit," I said, "done turned that young girl's head.

Daddy always says if you give a man a white shirt and a tie and a suit of clothes, you can find out real quick how sorry he is. Daddy says it's the quickest way to find out."

"Do her daddy know she's messing round with him?"

"Shore he knows. A man allus knows what his youngun is doing. Special if she's a girl." I flipped back to the man in the red hunting jacket and the wading boots. "You see them shotguns behind him there on the wall? Them his guns. That second one right there, see that one, the double barrel? That gun is loaded with double-ought buckshot. You know how come it loaded?"

"He gone stop that fooling around," said Willalee.

And so we sat there on the porch with the pots and pans banging back in the house over the iron stove and Lottie Mae there in the door where she had come to stand and listen to us as we talked even though we would not let her help with the story. And before it was over, we had discovered all the connections possible between the girl in the step-ins and the young man in the knife-creased suit and the older man in the red hunting jacket with the shotguns on the wall behind him. And more than that we also discovered that the man's kin people, when they had found out about the trouble he was having with his daughter and the young man, had plans of their own to fix it so the high sheriff wouldn't even have to know about it. They were going to set up and wait on him to take a shoat hog out of another field, and when he did, they'd be waiting with their own guns and knives (which we stumbled upon in another part of the catalogue) and they was gonna throw down on him and see if they couldn't make two pieces out of him instead of one. We had in the story what they thought and what they said and what they felt and why they didn't think that the young man, as good as he looked and as well as he stood in his fancy clothes, would ever straighten out and become the man the daddy wanted for his only daughter.

Before it was over, we even had the girl in the step-ins fixing it so that the boy in the suit could be shot. And by the time my family and Willalee's family came walking down the road from the tobacco field toward the house, the entire Wish Book was filled with feuds of every kind and violence, maimings, and all the other vicious happenings of the world.

Since where we lived and how we lived was almost hermetically sealed from everything and everybody else, fabrication became a way of life. Making up stories, it seems to me now, was not only a way for us to understand the way we lived but also a defense against it. It was no doubt the first step in a life devoted primarily to men and women and children who never lived anywhere but in my imagination. I have found in them infinitely more order and beauty and satisfaction than I ever have in the people who move about me in the real world. And Willalee Bookatee and his family were always there with me in those first tentative steps. God knows what it would have been like if it had not been for Willalee and his people, with whom I spent nearly as much time as I did with my own family.

There was a part of me in which it did not matter at all that they were black, but there was another part of me in which it had to matter because it mattered to the world I lived in. It mattered to my blood. It is easy to remember the morning I found out Willalee was a nigger.

It was not very important at the time. I do not know why I have remembered it so vividly and so long. It was the tiniest of moments that slipped by without anybody marking it or thinking about it.

It was later in the same summer I awoke to a knowledge of myself in the enormous, curving oak roots. It was Sunday, bright and hot, and we were on the way to church. Everybody except daddy, who was sick from whiskey. But he would not have gone even if he were well. The few times he ever did go he could never stand more than five or ten minutes of the sermon before he quietly went out a side door to stand beside the pickup truck smoking hand-rolled Prince Albert cigarettes until it was all over.

An aunt, her husband, and their children had come by to take us to the meeting in their car. My aunt was a lovely, gentle lady whom I loved nearly as much as mama. I was out on the porch waiting for my brother to get ready. My aunt stood beside me, pulling on the thin black gloves she wore to church winter and summer. I was talking nonstop, which I did even as a child, telling her a story—largely made up—about what happened to me and my brother the last time we went to town.

Robert Jones figured in the story. Robert Jones was a black man who lived in Bacon County. Unlike any other black man I knew of, though, he owned a big farm with a great shining house on it. He had two sons who were nearly seven feet tall. They were all known as very hard workers. I had never heard anybody speak of Robert Jones and his family with anything but admiration.

". . . so me and Hoyet was passing the cotton gin and Mr. Jones was standing there with his wife and. . . ."

My aunt leaned down and put her arm around my shoulders. Her great soft breast pressed warmly at my ear. She said: "No, son. Robert Jones is a nigger. You don't say 'mister' when you speak of a nigger. You don't say 'Mr. Jones,' you say 'nigger Jones.'"

I never missed a stroke in my story. ". . . so me and him was passing the cotton gin and nigger Jones was standing there with his wife. . . ."

We were all dutiful children in Bacon County, Georgia.

I don't know what difference it ever made that I found out Willalee Bookatee was a nigger. But no doubt it made a difference. Willalee was our friend, my brother's and mine, but we sometimes used him like a toy. He was always a surefire cure for boredom because among other things he could be counted on to be scared witless at the mention of a bull. How many afternoons would have been endless if we couldn't have said to one another: "Let's go get Willalee Bookatee and scare the shit out of him."

It didn't take much encouragement or deception to get Willalee out in the cornfield with us just after noon, when it was hot as only a day can be hot in the middle of an airless field in Georgia.

Hoyet turned to Willalee Bookatee and said: "You ever seen this here bull?"

"Which air bull?" Willalee rolled his eyes and shuffled his feet and looked off down the long heat-distorted rows of corn, the corn so green it seemed almost purple in the sun.

"The bull that stays in this field," I said.

My brother said: "To hook little boys that won't tote a citron."

Willalee was out in the middle of a twenty-acre field of corn, equidistant from all fences, brought there by design by Hoyet and me to see if we could make him carry a heavy citron to the gate. A citron is a vine that grows wild in the field, and it puts out a fruit which is also called a citron and looks in every way like a watermelon except it's slightly smaller. Its rind was sometimes pickled and used in fruitcakes, but by and large, it was a worthless plant and farmers did everything they could think of to get rid of them, but they somehow always managed to survive.

"Hook little boys," said Willalee.

It wasn't a question; it was only repeated into the quiet dust-laden air. There had been no rain in almost two weeks, and when you stepped between the corn rows, the dust rose and hung, not falling or blowing in the windless day, but simply hanging interminably between the purple shucks of corn.

"No siree, it's got to be bigger than that one," I said when Willalee rushed to snatch a grapefruit-sized citron off the ground. "That old bull wants you to tote one bigger'n that."

Willalee was scared to death of bulls. He had been trampled and caught on the horns of one when he was about three years old, and he never got over it. At the mention of a bull, Willalee would go gray and his eyes would get a little wild and sometimes he would get out of control with his fear. Willalee was struggling with an enormous citron, staggering in the soft dirt between the corn rows.

"That's better," I said. "That's a lot better. That old bull will never touch you with that in your arms."

Willalee couldn't have weighed more than about sixty-five pounds, and the citron he caught against his skinny chest must have weighed twenty pounds.

"How come it is you ain't got no citron?" said Willalee.

My brother and I walked on either side of him. He could hardly see over the citron he was carrying.

"We already carried ourn," I said. "That bull don't make you tote but one. After you tote one citron, you can take and come out here in the field anytime you want to and that bull don't pay no more mind than if you was a goat."

Willalee was a long way from the gate, and he had already started crying, soundlessly, tears tracking down through the dust on his cheeks. That citron was hurting him a lot.

"But you ain't toted your citron yet," I said, "and that big bull looking to hook into your ass if you put it down, that bull looking to hook him some ass, some good tender little-boy ass, cause that the kind he likes the best."

"I know," whispered Willalee through his tears. "I know he do."

And so Willalee made it to the fence with his citron and felt himself forever safe from the bull. He didn't hesitate at the fence but went right over it, still carrying his citron in case the bull was watching, and once over it, he didn't say anything but took off in a wild run down the road.

CHAPTER 5

But Willalee was not entirely helpless, and he gave back about as good as he got. He once took a crabapple and cut the core out of it, put some cow plop down in the bottom of the hole, and then covered it over all around the top with some blackberry jam his mama had canned.

"Jam in a apple?" I said.

"Bes thing *you* ever put in your mouth," he said.

My brother, who had seen him fix the apple, stood there and watched him offer it to me, did in fact encourage me to take it.

"Had one myself," he said. "That thing is some gooooood eatin."

"I ain't had nair one with jam in it," I said.

"Take you a great big bite," said Willalee.

I not only took a great big bite, I took *two* great big bites, getting right down to the bottom. Anybody else would have known what he was eating after the first bite. It took me two. Even then, I did not so much taste it as I smelled it.

"I believe this thing is ruint," I said.

"Nawwwww," said Willalee.

"Nawwwww," said my brother.

"It smells just like . . . like. . . ." And then I knew what he had fed me.

Willalee was laughing when he should have been running. I got him around the neck and we both went into the dust, where we wallowed around for a while before my brother got tired of watching it and pulled us apart. No matter what we did to one another, though, Willalee and I never stayed angry at each other for more than an hour or two, and I always felt welcome at his family's house. Whatever I am, they had a large part in making. More, I am convinced Willalee's grandma, Auntie, made the best part of me. She was thin and brittle with age, and her white hair rode her fleshless face like a cap. From daylight to dark she kept a thick cud of snuff working in her caving, toothless mouth, and she was expert at sending streams of brown spit great distances into tin cans.

The inside of their tiny house was dark on the brightest day and smelled always of ashes, even in the summer. Auntie did not like much light inside the house, so most of the time she kept the curtains drawn, curtains she had made from fertilizer sacks and decorated with bits of colored cloth. Bright light was for the outside, she said, and shade—the more the better—was for the inside.

I ate with them often, as often as mama would let me, and the best thing I ever got from their table was possum, which we *never* got at home because mama would not cook it. She said she knew it would taste like a wet dog smells. But it did not. Auntie could cook it in a way that would break your heart. Willalee and I would stand about in her dark, ash-smelling little kitchen and watch her prepare it. She would scald and scrape it just like you would scald and scrape a hog, gut it, remove the eyes, which she always carefully set aside in a shallow dish. The head, except for the eyes, would be left intact. After she parboiled it an hour and a half, she would take out the teeth, stuff the little body with sweet potatoes, and then bake the whole thing in the oven for two hours.

The reason mama would never cook a possum, of course, was because a possum is just like a buzzard. It will eat anything that is dead. The longer dead the better. It was not unusual to come across a cow that had been dead in the woods for three or four days and see a possum squeezing out of the swollen body after having eaten a bellyful of rotten flesh. But it never occurred to me to think of that when we all sat down to the table and waited for Willalee's daddy to say the only grace he ever said: "Thank the Lord for this food."

The first possum I ever shared with them was in that first summer in my memory of myself, and with the possum we had fresh sliced tomatoes and steamed okra—as well as fried okra—and corn on the cob, butter beans, fried pork, and biscuits made out of flour and water and lard.

Because I was company, Auntie gave me the best piece: the head. Which had a surprising amount of meat on it and in it. I ate around on the face for a while, gnawing it down to the cheekbones, then ate the tongue, and finally went into the skull cavity for the brains, which Auntie had gone to some pains to explain was the best part of the piece.

After we finished the possum, Willalee and Lottie Mae and I stayed at the table sopping cane syrup with biscuits. Will and Katie had gone out on the front porch to rest, and we were left alone with Auntie, who was already working over the table, taking plates to the tin tub where she would wash them, and putting whatever food had been left over into the screen-wire safe.

Finally, she came to stand beside where I sat at the table. "Come on now, boy," she said, "an ole Auntie'll show you."

"Show me what?" I said.

She was holding the little shallow saucer with the possum's eyes in it. The eyes were clouded in a pink pool of diluted blood. They rolled on the saucer as I watched.

"Nem mind," she said. "Come on."

We followed her out the back door into the yard. We didn't go but a step or two before she squatted down and dug a hole. The rear of the house was almost covered with stretched and nailed hides of squirrels and rabbits and coons and even a fox which Willalee's daddy had trapped. I would find out later that Auntie had tanned the hides by rubbing the animals' hides on the flesh side with their own brains. It caused the hair to fall out of the hide and left it soft and pliable.

"You eat a possum, you bare its eyes," she said, still squatting beside the little hole she had dug.

I motioned toward Sam where he stood at my heels. "You gone bury it," I said, "you better bury it deeper'n that. Don't he'll dig it up. You might as well go on and give it to'm now."

"Won't dig up no possum's eyes," she said. "Sam's got good sense."

Sam did not, either.

"Know how come you got to barum?" she said.

"How come?" I said.

"Possums eat whatall's dead," she said. Her old, cracked voice had gone suddenly deep and husky. "You gone die too, boy."

"Yes," I said, stunned.

"You be dead an in the ground, but you eat this possum an he gone come lookin for you. He ain't ever gone stop lookin for you."

I could not now speak. I watched as she carefully took the two little clouded eyes out of the dish and placed them in the hole, arranging them so they were looking straight up toward the cloudless summer sky. They seemed to watch me where I was.

Auntie smiled, showing her snuff-colored gums. "You ain't got to think on it, boy. See, we done put them eyes looking up. But you gone be *down*. Ain't never gone git you. Possum be looking for you up, an you gone be six big feets under the ground. You gone allus be all right, you put the eyes lookin up."

Auntie made me believe we live in a discoverable world, but that most of what we discover is an unfathomable mystery that we can name—even defend against—but never understand.

My fifth birthday had come and gone, and it was the middle of the summer, 1940, hot and dry and sticky, the air around the table thick with the droning of house flies. At supper that night neither my brother nor I had to ask where daddy was. There was always, when he had gone for whiskey, a tension in the house that you could breathe in with the air and feel on the surface of your skin, and more than that, there was that awful look on mama's face. I suppose the same look was on our faces, too, worried as we all were, not knowing what the night would bring, not knowing if it would be this night or the next night, or the morning following the second night, when he would come home after a drunk, bloodied, his clothes stinking with whiskey sweat.

We sat at the supper table, eating quietly, nobody saying a word, and when we finished, my brother and I went just as quietly into the fireroom and sat in ladder-back chairs, staring into the cold hearthstone where there had been no fire for two months. By the time mama came in to sit with us we had already brought in the foot tub full of water. The only thing we seemed to wash for long periods of time on the farm was our face and hands at the water shelf on the back porch and our feet in front of the hearthstone.

That night as we sat silently together, everybody thinking of daddy, thinking of where he was and how he might come home, I—for reasons which I'll never know—turned to mama and said: "I want to preach."

She immediately understood that I didn't mean that I wanted to be a preacher or to become a preacher, but rather that I wanted to preach right then. She said: "Well, son, if you want to preach, just get up there and preach to us."

She was always open and direct with us, always kind and loving, even though she was always strict. She believed that if a child did something he knew was wrong, had been told was wrong, he had to be whipped. And she did throughout my childhood throw some pretty good whippings on my brother and me. But she never whipped us when we did not know that we deserved it and, more, when we did not expect it.

Mama and my brother sat there in front of the cold fireplace while I got up and turned my ladder-back chair over and got the crocheted doily off the pedal-driven Singer sewing machine to cover the chair with. The chair covered with the doily made a fine altar from which to preach. I took hold of it with both hands, looked out at them, and started my sermon.

I said: "We all of us made out of dirt. God took Him up some dirt and put it in his hands and rolled it around and then he spit in the dirt and roll it some more and out of that dirt and God spit, he made you and me, all of us."

That is the way my preaching began. I don't remember how it ended, but I know it went on for a long time and it was made pretty much out of what I had heard in church, what I had heard the preacher say about hell and God and heaven and damnation and the sorry state of the human condition. Hell was at the center of any sermon I had ever heard in Bacon County. In all the churches, you smelled the brimstone and the sulfur and you felt the fire and you were made to know that because of what you had done in your life, you were doomed forever. Unless somehow, somewhere, you were touched by the action of mercy and the Grace of God. But you could not, you must not, count on the Grace of God. It probably would not come to you because you were too sorry.

I was exhausted by the time it was over, and I was asleep the moment my head touched the pillow. But I heard the pickup truck when it came in. And I heard daddy come through the front gate, the plow points banging and his own drunk-heavy feet on the steps and the front door slamming, and then I heard, as I already knew I would, querulous voices as mama and daddy confronted each other there beyond the thin wall. Finally, their voices raised to shouts and even screams, but since there was nothing breaking, no pots hitting the wall, no glass splattering on the floor, no furniture turning over, I could stand lying in my bed if I concentrated on hell and damnation. This was nothing compared to the eternal fires of hell that God might someday demand that I endure. With my whole self firmly immersed in hell, I could usually go back to sleep.

I woke up sometime in the middle of the night. An enormous and brilliant moon shone over the cotton field where I was standing, still in my gown. It was not a dream and I knew immediately that it was not a dream. I was where I thought I was, and I had come here by walking in my sleep. I came awake that night the way I always have when I've gotten up in my sleep and walked. Terrified. Terrified almost beyond terror because it had no name and was sourceless. My heart was pounding, and my gown was soaked with sweat and sticking to my freezing skin. My mouth was full of the taste of blood where I'd chewed my lips.

The cotton bolls were open all about me. As far as I could see, all the way to the dark wall of trees surrounding the field, was a white sheet of cotton, brilliant and undulating under the heavy moon. I stood there for a long time, unable to move. Off there to the left was the enormous oak tree that I had slept under that morning, it, too, brilliant in the moon, and behind the tree was the house, dark in its own shadow. I did not know what to do. I did not cry and I did not scream. I did not think that I could go back there to the dark house where my family slept. I somehow knew they would not receive me. I knew that I was guilty of something neither man nor God could forgive. But it would always be so when I walked in my sleep.

I stood utterly still and waited because I knew if I waited long enough, the terror would find a source and a name. Once it had a name, no matter how awful, I would be able to live with it. I could go back home.

Gradually, the terror shapes itself into a school bus. I can see it plainly. It is full of children. Stopped by the side of a road. I am in the ditch by the side of the road. They do not see me. It is broad daylight and many of the children are looking right at me. But they don't—they can't—see me. I have something in my hand. I do not know what it is. I cannot tell what it is. I come slowly out of the ditch and touch the school bus with the thing in my hand. The moment contact is made, the whole bus disintegrates in my eyes. There is no explosion, no sound at all. The disintegration is silent as sleep. When I can see again, the bus is on its back, broken children hang from open windows, and some—the ones toward the back—are drenched in gas from the ruptured tank and they are frying, noiselessly frying. I can smell them frying. And I am terrified at the probable consequences that will follow what I have done, but I am glad I have done it.

Now I can go home, and I start off in a dead run between the rows of cotton toward the dark house beyond the oak tree.

When I got to the door, I opened it quietly and went down the hall to the little room where I knew daddy was sleeping on a pallet. It was where he often had to sleep when he came in drunk and out of control and mama would not let him into their room. He lay, still dressed, curled on the quilt spread across the floor under an open window through which bright moonlight fell. I sat down beside him and touched his face, traced the thick scar of perfect teeth on his flat high cheekbone. The air in the room was heavy with the sweet smell of bourbon whiskey. Sweat stood on his forehead and darkly stained his shirt.

"Daddy," I said. He made a small noise deep in his chest, and his eyes opened. "Daddy, I'm scared."

He pushed himself onto one elbow and put an arm around me and drew me against him. I could feel the bristle of his beard on my neck. I trembled and tried not to cry.

"Sho now," he whispered against my ear. "Everybody's scared now and then."

"I was in the cotton field," I said. "Out there."

He turned his head, and we both looked through the window at the flat white field of cotton shining under the moon.

"You was dreaming, boy," he said. "But you all right now."

"I woke up out there." Now I was crying, not making any noise, but unable to keep the tears from streaming down my face. I pushed my bare feet into the moonlight. "Look," I said. My feet and the hem of my gown were gray with the dust of the field.

He drew back and looked into my eyes, smiling. "You walked in your sleep. It ain't nothing to worry about. You probably got it from me. I'as bad to walk in my sleep when I was a boy."

The tears eased back. "You was?" I said.

"Done it a lot," he said. "Don't mean nothing."

I don't know if he was telling the truth. But hearing him say it was something that he had done and that I might have got it from him took my fear away.

"You lie down here on the pallet with your ole daddy and go to sleep. Me an you is all right. We *both* all right."

I lay down with my head on his thick arm, wrapped in the warm, sweet smell of whiskey and sweat, and was immediately asleep.

Willalee's daddy did not drink and almost never left the farm. In fantasy I often thought of Willalee as my brother, thought of his family as my family. His daddy was always there, and everybody in the family had a place and purpose, all of them integrated into the business of making a living in a way that my family was not. My own daddy was easy to love, but he was often drunk and often gone, Willalee's daddy was easy to love, too, because everywhere about the farm he was there, always steady, never raising his voice, making you feel good to be with him. He never told anybody to do anything. He asked for your help in a way that made you feel as though you were helping him out of a tight spot he could not get out of by himself.

"Reckon you boys could bring Sam and help me doctor a cow?"

Willalee's daddy had stopped us in the lane between the house and the mule lot. We were in a little two-wheeled buggy pulled by Old Black Bill, the boss goat of the herd we kept. Willalee sat beside me holding two blackbirds we had just taken out of a trap down behind the field.

"Harry got to put up these 'er buds," said Willalee.

"That be fine," Will said. "I be in the lot."

Willalee and I had been down to my bird trap that Saturday afternoon in late July and found the two blackbirds in it. Sometimes the trap would take a whole covey of quail, as many as thirteen or fourteen birds at one time. My Grandma Hazelton taught me how to make it out of tobacco sticks. Those are the sticks, about six feet long and one inch square, that the tobacco is strung on to be hung in the barn and cooked. To make the trap you lay the sticks down, one on top of another with the ends overlapping like the walls of a log cabin. When the four sides of the trap are about eighteen or twenty inches high, you cover it straight across the top, leaving about an inch between the sticks. Now you've got a cage six feet square that admits the sun well enough for it to be nearly as light inside as it is outside. For good reason. Birds won't enter a dark trap.

You dig a hole—a rather large hole—under one side of the square of tobacco sticks. Sprinkle meal or broken corn around the front of the trap, some more down in the hole you've dug under one side, and still more inside the trap itself. Birds will come along, eat a little outside, scratch and feed into the hole, and finally go up into the trap where most of the food has been placed. When they get ready to leave, they will never once think of the hole right there at their feet. They could walk out the same way they came in, but when they get ready to go, their only thought is flight.

It always took some doing to get the birds out of the trap, and that morning was no exception. You had to be really careful when you were working with a trap that big or your birds would get away. After a half hour of false starts, we finally got the two blackbirds out and we were taking them up to the house to turn them loose in the little room at the back of the house mama had given over to my brother and me. The room had always been empty except for a couple of broken chairs and half a bedstead, so my brother and I asked her one day if we could have it to keep birds in, and to our complete amazement, she said yes.

Birds, particularly wild birds, are a little crazy when you turn them loose in a room. But if there are other birds already resting quietly in the room, they don't fly blindly about, bashing into walls and windows. The floor was ankle deep in straw and leaves and twigs and moss for the birds to build nests with in the dead, branching limbs I had nailed around the room. A pair of redbirds I caught built a nest, laid eggs, and hatched them out.

After we turned the blackbirds loose, I was about to put down meal and corn and peas and fresh water when I saw that my brother had already done it. We never had gotten the ownership of the room straight. He said it was his because he took care of the birds. I said it was mine because I took care of the birds. Mama said it belonged to us both and that neither one of us took care of the birds.

When we had gotten rid of the birds, Willalee and I went back out to help Will with the cow that had screwworms. He had her penned behind the corncrib and he was waiting for us there, squatting on his heels in the shade of the fence, watching the cow. She was so poor you could hang your hat on her hipbone. Her lifeless hide cleaved to her ribs and hung in folds down to her widened, shriveled udder which had been torn on one side and was now alive with worms. She backed into a corner of the lot when she saw us, head lowered, showing us the points of her long sweeping horns.

Sam had come with us, and it was up to him to take her down so we could clean her out. If we didn't, the screwworms would very likely kill her. Screwworms are gone now, but when I was a boy, they were just about everywhere. If any animal got a cut on it from something like barbed wire or in any other way managed to tear its hide in the hot months of the year, a blue-bellied fly about half as big as a man's fingernail would blow eggs into the wound. From the eggs would come tiny worms, hundreds, sometimes thousands of them. The worms could, and often did, kill whatever animal they got into. The only two things on a farm I never saw screwworms in were chickens and people.

Will left the shade of the fence and came to stand between us. He put his left hand on his son's shoulder and his right hand on my shoulder. I could feel it thick and strong and warm through my shirt. I thought of that morning when my own daddy had put his hand, the same kind of strong, thick hand, on my shoulder. But with his other hand he had wiped his forehead and I'd watched the sweat drip from the ends of his fingers. He had laughed when he said: "Boy, that's pure bourbon whiskey running off my hand." But I had not laughed as I watched him get in the pickup truck and drive off. And now I pretended the hand on my shoulder was his.

"I don't know what that ole cow'd do if you boys didn't help me doctor'er." He sucked his lips and clucked to Sam, his voice coming now low as a whisper. "Sic'er. Take'er down, Sam."

Sam was as good a catch dog as anybody ever saw work. He circled to the cow's left, cautiously, growling but not barking. He had to first get her out of the corner, if he was to catch her. We backed out of the lot into the space between the stables and corncrib.

Almost gently, and without seeming effort, Sam soon had the cow trotting round and round, then running as fast as she could given the tight circle she had to make in the lot. He was running right beside her, step for step, when he lunged and caught her high in the right ear. As soon as he had a firm hold, he drew his big body upward. His weight pulled her head down and he went between her front feet. The cow was thrown in a single solid *thump* onto her back. Stunned, the breath partially knocked out of her, she lay as still as if she were dead.

Sam was a choke dog as well as a catch dog. On command, he would attempt to catch anything, even a mule. But once he took hold there were only two ways to get him off. He always kept his eyes tightly shut, and he seemed to go stone deaf as soon as he caught. Then it was either take him by the throat and choke him off or else pry his mouth open with a little spoon-shaped piece of wood whittled from a shingle.

Will twisted her head until he could brace against her top horn with his leg. He poured the Benzol into the wound, and it worked alive with squirming worms, boiling them out onto the hide. Then he took a fork that was kept with the Benzol and carefully cleaned out the V-shaped wound. The last thing that was applied was a thick, black, turpentine-smelling paste that sealed the hide so it would not be reinfected.

"I reckon she'll live," he said.

We untied the cow's legs and stood back as the cow got shakily to her feet. Will's shirt was soaking wet halfway to his belt, and sweat ran on his forehead and dripped from his chin.

When we had finished with the cow, Will took us back down to the tenant house, where we cut a watermelon and sat on the front porch eating it while Auntie banged around in the kitchen making supper.

CHAPTER 6

The first real illness of my life came on the night of August 7, 1940, exactly three months after my fifth birthday. The day will always be fixed firmly in memory because it was the day the Jew came. He came into our little closed world smelling of strangeness and far places. Willalee and I had just come up from his house when we saw him far off down the road coming steadily and slowly, dust rising behind his wagon in the heat-distorted distance. My brother came out to join us where we stood under the oak tree.

The Jew traveled in a covered wagon pulled by a pair of mismatched mare mules. One of the mules was normal-sized, but the other one was small enough to be a pony, although she was not. The tiny mule had a cast in one eye, and her left ear had been split all the way down to her head so it made her look like she had three ears.

The Jew, whose name I never knew, always dressed in black, and on even the hottest days he wore heavy black pants and a black coat and a little black cap right on top of his head. He traveled a regular route through Appling County and Pierce County and Jeff Davis County and Bacon County. People said you could set your watch by where he was on any given day of the month, so regularly did he travel his route.

The inside of his wagon was better than anything Willalee and I could make up, filled as it was with spools of thread and needles and thimbles and bolts of cloth and knives and forks and spoons—some new, some used—and a grinding stone of a special design so that he could sharpen anything, and mule harness, and staples, and nails, and a thousand other things.

He did business almost exclusively with women, and whatever they needed, they could always find in the Jew's wagon. If they didn't have the money to pay for what they needed, he would trade for eggs or chickens or cured meat or canned vegetables and berries.

He had a water barrel strapped to the back of his wagon, and hanging from the sides of the canvas cover and from the sides of the wooden body of the wagon were frying pans and boiling pots and even washtubs and cast-iron washpots. He had also contrived to wire mason fruit jars onto the side of his wagon, wire them in such a way that when they swung they would not strike each other and break.

I can never remember anybody saying anything bad about him or anybody treating him badly. But he *was* different from the rest of us. When he spoke, he did not sound like us. For that reason he was mysterious and often used to scare the children with. People in the county would sometimes say to an unruly child: "If you don't behave, youngun, I just might let you go on off with the Jew. Just let'm have you." It was at least as effective as a whipping.

He came slowly into the lane in front of the house and stopped his wagon under the oak tree. Willalee, my brother, and I stood in the dust watching him. He had longer hair than we had ever seen on a man and a long dirty-white beard. The fingers on his hands were badly twisted. We wanted very badly to speak to him, to talk to him, but we were afraid. After the dust had settled under his wagon and he had been sitting there a long quiet time, he slowly turned his head, looked at us, nodded his head in the smallest of movements, and got stiffly down by stepping over onto the hub of the wheel.

Mama came out of the house with a pair of scissors in her hand. He stood by his wagon, and when she was near, he moved his head forward in a slight, stiff bow instead of taking off his hat as other men might have done. He did not speak.

"I got these for you to sharpen," mama said.

He took the scissors from her and turned them slowly in his hands. Then: "For maybe a quarter?" he said, looking up from the scissors through his heavy eyebrows.

"I thought a dime," mama said.

"For less than fifteen cents I couldn't," he said.

"I guess it's worth that to me," said mama.

"In the wagon," he said, "I have some very good cloth. A nice bright print."

"I ain't got the money," mama said, but she turned her eyes toward the back of the wagon.

"Let me show you," he said. "It does no harm to look."

"It don't do no good neither, if you ain't got the money," she said.

But he was already starting for the back of the wagon, and she followed him. He opened one flap on the back and pulled a thin bolt of thin, brightly colored cloth halfway out and spread a small length of it over his hands.

"Feel it," he said. "A very nice cloth."

"I ain't got the money," she said. But she felt the cloth anyway, slowly, letting it trail through her fingers.

"Maybe some corn for my animals," he said, "and a little hay."

"We didn't make much hay this year," she said. "We ain't got nigh enough for the stock on the place now."

"You wouldn't miss fifty ears of corn and two bats of hay," he said. "For that much, I could maybe let you have three yards. It's very good cloth."

"It ain't worth fifty ears and that much hay to me," she said. "We didn't make much hay this year."

"Fifty-five ears then," he said, "and one bat of hay."

"I might could see my way clear to let you have forty-five ears and a bat," she said.

"It is very little for such nice cloth," he said. He looked into the darkness of the covered wagon for a moment as if expecting to find some answer in there. "But for you, why not a bargain?"

The expression on his face never changed while they talked. Mama left the scissors with him and went back into the house. He took his team out and led them to the lot and watered them at the trough. We followed him and watched as he put the corn and hay into a burlap sack. He did it all very slowly and with great deliberation. He never seemed sad and he never seemed happy. He did not speak to us, nor we to him. He spoke only when he was trading and then only so much as was necessary to business. He did all that he did in seeming exhaustion, but with utter patience.

We watched him wash his face and hands in the water trough at the lot, and then we watched as he put his team back to the wagon. His twisted hands worked quickly and surely over the scissors at his grinding stone. Mama came back out and watched him cut the bolt of cloth with the scissors he had sharpened. When he finished, she silently took two brown chicken eggs out of her apron and gave them to him. Just as silently he took them and stood holding them in his hand as though weighing them.

"I thought you might could use them," she said.

He nodded silently and then turned and slowly reached deep into the back of his wagon and finally came out with three tiny peppermint balls. He opened his hand to Willalee, my brother, and me. The candy lay in his palm unwrapped and dusted with confectionery sugar.

"For you, and you, and you," he said, giving each of us a candy.

He turned to my mother, gave his slight, stiff bow, and climbed over the wheel and onto the seat board of his wagon. When he lifted the lines, his pair of mismatched mules leaned into their collars and he was moving away. With the candies melting on our tongues, we stood and watched him go, feeling as though we had ourselves just been on a long trip, a trip to the world we knew was out there but had never seen.

That night I woke up with a burning fever. Mama, as was her custom when treating toothache, fever, sore throat, earache, eye strain, or headache, sent my brother down to the tenant house to get some wool. When my brother knocked on Auntie's door in the middle of the night, she would know immediately what he was there for, and without turning on a light she would stand in her gown in the doorway lighted bright as day by the moon and with a pair of heavy scissors cut two thimble-sized pieces out of her hair.

Mama said the wool from Auntie's head kept our ears warm and the oil from it eased the pain. Sometimes it seemed to help, sometimes not. This time it did not. The next morning the wool was still in my ears tighter than ever because she had pushed it deeper into my head every hour or two, but I still had the fever and my legs had begun to draw up. They were bent at the knees, and the ligaments were slowly drawing my heels closer and closer to the cheeks of my buttocks. It felt like both legs were knotted from hip to heel. The pain was enough to make me chew my lips and the inside of my mouth.

Daddy got home, sick himself and seriously hung-over, just in time to drive to the only farm I knew of in the county that had a telephone. The man who owned it didn't really farm the way the rest of us did. His farming was done in the woods. He had a big turpentine distillery and a good-sized village of blacks living on his place. The blacks cut V's into the faces of pine trees and nailed tin cups under the V's to catch the raw turpentine when it drained out. They collected the turpentine in buckets, which they poured into barrels, which eventually found their way, usually on mule-drawn sleds, to the distillery.

Daddy called Dr. Sharp, who arrived at about noon looking starched and powerful as God as he always did, dressed in his black coat and carrying his black bag full of magic. It wasn't long though before he looked as I had never seen him. He had determined with pins that there was feeling in both legs. But that was about as far as he got, which he freely admitted. He scratched his head and poked here and pulled there and finally said he didn't know for sure what I had, but he thought it was infantile paralysis.

He left something for the pain and said he would be back out the next day. By the time he got back my legs were drawn as tight as they were going to get—as tight as they *could* get, with the heels pulled all the way up until they touched the backs of my thighs. Dr. Sharp even had Dr. Branch to come over from Baxley. But he was as baffled as Dr. Sharp. I got a few shots for the pain, and both Dr. Branch and Dr. Sharp said I would never walk again. It was a time of great grief for mama and a time of sheer terror for me because I could not imagine what in God's name I would do for the rest of my life with my legs drawn up that way.

As it happens, about four days later, a band of gypsies came through in their wagons. It was not uncommon to see them traveling about the countryside, doing whatever they were allowed to do: repairing pots and pans and tubs, trading, doing a little carpentry—mostly roofs of barns and lots. But mostly they stole. At least most of the farmers were convinced they did.

Like the Jew, they dressed differently from the way we dressed, and they spoke to us in voices full of accents different from our own, at times spoke a language amongst themselves that made as much sense to us as the greaseless squealing of a wagon wheel. And because of their language and the way they dressed, we thought they had powers we did not have: powers for curses, potions, and various miraculous cures that could be had for a little money or a few chickens.

The head of the tribe, a very old man who looked strangely like the Jew even though he was not bearded and wore a bright cloth on his head instead of a black cap, had heard that I was sick and asked to be taken into the house to see me. He said he might be able to help me, said he might have something in his bag that could kill the disease, attack it and kill it. He had a bag just like the doctor's, except the old gypsy's was made out of the hide of a goat from which the hair had not been removed.

While the old man was looking at me, touching my legs and head in a tentative way, stopping now and again to search through his goatskin medicine bag and eventually selling a bag of herbs for $10—a sizable amount of money then—while he was doing that, the rest of the band went out to the lot and stole a brood sow. A theft we did not discover until the next morning.

I drank those herbs boiled in tea for ten days, but when I had finished, my heels were just as tight against my ass as they had ever been. We were out $10 and a brood sow.

Following the gypsy came a great parade of people: aunts and uncles and cousins and even Grandpa and Grandma Hazelton, who didn't get out of the house much anymore because they were full of years and had the miseries; and people from neighboring farms; and after them, total strangers from other counties, all of them come to stare at me where I lay in a high fever and filled with the most awful cramps, come to stare at my rigid legs. I knew that they were staring with unseemly intensity at my legs, that they wanted most of all to touch them, and I hated it and dreaded it and was humiliated by it. I felt how lonely and savage it was to be a freak.

Sometime later, the fourth or fifth day of my illness, after Dr. Sharp and Dr. Branch both had come and after both of them had said they did not know for sure what was wrong but thought (the thought voiced in front of me) that I would never walk again and after my uncle had come—the one who spoke in tongues—after he had fallen on me in a fit of glossolalia, which did not seem to affect me one way or the other, there appeared at my bedside a faith healer brought in from another county, Jeff Davis. He stood by my bed for what seemed to me a very long time. He was a small man with an upper lip so long that you could not see his top teeth and very few of his lower ones. The flapping upper lip made him appear toothless, and he never took his hat off.

He seemed to me the most objective of men. What he knew he knew with the certitude of science. When he spoke of what he could do, it sounded like the recitation of fact. It did not trouble him in the least if you did not believe he could do what he said he could do. Such doubts were met with a numbing indifference.

"I can cure the thrash out of a youngun's mouth," he said, still looking at me.

"He ain't *got* the thrash," daddy said, a raging unbeliever at the foot of the bed.

"It is red thrash and yeller thrash and black thrash," he said. "Yeller thrash is the worst."

"It's a God's pity that ain't what he's got," daddy said.

"God," he said quiet as a whisper but full of fact. "God? Did you say God? It's the way I do it. With the help of the

Lord. With the help of the Lord. I couldn't do no healing without the help of the Lord."

Daddy snorted. He had a way of making it sound just like a
horse does after he's had a run. I had heard him and mama arguing about whether or not to bring the faith healer. The argument was resolved when he found out it was not going to cost
anything. "Labor deserves its hire," he would say, "but them
sumbitches don't do nothing."

When somebody said in his presence that a preacher had
made a good sermon on a particular Sunday, he would invari-
ably say that he could make a good sermon, too, if somebody
would give him a week's wages to do it. "Purty goddamn good
wages for a hour's work."

Mama brought a ladder-back chair to the side of the bed
and then retreated into the shadows beyond the reach of the
kerosene lamp. The faith healer sat down in the chair and
carefully adjusted his hat until it was squared to his satisfaction.
Now that he was sitting, the baggy, folding trousers and the
heavy coat did not look as if there was really a body in them,
only maybe a lot of old coat hangers. Also, I now saw that
he was a little walleyed, but as best he could, he still fixed me
with a steady stare. I remember thinking (thinking in anger,
which in turn came out of fear) that if he was a healer, the first
thing he ought to do is go look in a mirror and heal that wan-
dering eye. But of course, I said nothing about it.

I did not know this man, not his name (although it was
mumbled to me), nor his work, and more than that, he was not
from our county, which amounted to making him not only a
stranger but a foreigner as well. I had had my legs stared at
now for days by a seemingly endless parade of people, and I
had been probed and pulled and finally pummeled by Dr.
Sharp and Dr. Branch, and I was still as bad off as ever. Nothing inspired me with any confidence, and certainly not this
little toothless, starved, and wrinkled man. He must have
known that I had no hope of him curing me because he sat and
talked to me for a long time in his flat, matter-of-fact way
about himself and his powers.

"I can draw far and I can stop blood," he said. "Why, it was one time, Tom, Tom's my middle youngun, Tom he got cut on the laig with a crosscut saw. They was a cuttin tobacker wood and he got cut on the laig with a crosscut saw and he was a bleeding bad. An when they come to me to go back down there in the woods where he was at cause he was hurt that bad, so bad he couldn't come back up to the house, when they come for me and I went down there, I just took one look at it.

"Didn't do a thing but look at it and said that verse out of Ezekiel. I said that verse and got that blood to stop right there where it was at.

"They'd been a puttin spider webs and I don't know what all up in that cut there trying to get it to stop. But it didn't stop till I got there, but when I got there and said the words, it stopped right away, youngun.

"Now the thing about far is you don't want to drive it no deeper. That's how come it is doctors cain't do no good with burns is they drive the far deeper. But me, what I do is draw it out, draw that far right on out of there. But a doctor he will most gently drive that heat right down to the bones, drive it even to the holler of the body. That far gets in the holler of the body, it'll jest cook an burn till it ain't nothin else to burn up anymore before it goes out. Which time you usually dead."

I could hear the rage mounting in my daddy's breathing at the foot of the bed. When the little man paused for breath, he said: "What about legs? Git to the part about legs."

Daddy's voice was full of helplessness and sarcasm and unbelieving, but if the faith healer heard the quality of the voice, he never let on that he did.

"You take them laigs of yorn right there," he said, pointing, as if there were some question as to which legs we were there to consider. "I cain't say as I ever seed laigs jest like them. But them is the Lord's laigs an He's seed them laigs and He's laid His hand on them laigs and He knows, so it don't bother me none that I ain't seed'm."

Daddy could not contain himself. "Then git to it," he shouted.

The little man turned his trowel-shaped face in the lamplight, and his steady voice, coming counterpoint to daddy's shout, seemed less than a whisper. "I already got to it. I'm through."

"Then why the hell ain't his legs done nothing?" asked daddy. "His legs is jest like they was."

"No, they ain't. They jest look like they was. I said the verse out of Ezekiel an now it is between me and that boy and the Lord. An it ain't any way his laigs is the way they was. Never be again, neither."

A long-drawn silence followed his words, and I felt, as well as saw, my daddy trembling as he watched my legs, watched them as if he expected them to suddenly and miraculously loosen and straighten. Insects fluttered through the screenless windows and burned instantly crisp against the lampshade as the room wavered in the guttering light. I was the focus of their attention, the little man's and mama's and even daddy's, as I realized that in his grief and however temporary, he was a believer.

As the silence stretched on, I was humiliated all over again because the action of mercy had not come down from God and touched my legs and made them well. They were just as bent and just as white and just as full of pain as they had ever been, and I thought about how it would be not only to suffer the whole world to look at how I was and find me freakish and unacceptable, but also to suffer the knowledge that God Himself would not intercede.

"His legs ain't done a goddamn thing," daddy said.

The little faith healer said, matter-of-factly: "You standin in danger of hellfire blasphemin when Ezekiel's spoke by mouth or mind."

Daddy did not say so much as sang in a lilting grief, his voice soft, the fight gone out of him: "My boy is crippled. A cripple."

The faith healer stood up. "He won't always be," he said, and without looking at me again left the room. Finally, from down the hall, his thin, tiny voice came floating back to us: "It mought be today, or it mought be tomorrow. Whatever it is God will allow."

That night, when all the lights were out and I was dozing

fitfully, daddy came into the room and lay down beside me. I could see well enough to see he was crying, crying in the open way that I had never seen a man cry.

"You want to sleep on your old daddy's arm, boy?"

When I slept with him, I always slept with my head on his arm. I lifted my head to his arm, and for the first time since the sickness started, I felt good.

"Why don't you tell me about the boy in the swamp?" I said.

It was a story he had told me many times before, always told in a different way from the way it had ever been told before but always about a boy who lived in a swamp and swam and fished and lay in the sun all day and had a best friend that was an alligator. I went to sleep trying to pretend that surely in the morning I would wake up and find my legs straightened. I tried to pretend that the last thing the faith healer had said from the hall had helped me to believe. God might not cure me that night, but tomorrow He would make it so I could walk again. And if not tomorrow, the next day. For a whole week I woke up every morning expecting my legs to be straight, expecting to be able to swing over to the side of the bed and stand up and go out and get my goat and Willalee Bookatee and the wagon. But it did not happen.

Finally, I quit believing that it would. Right there, as a child, I got to the bottom of what it means to be lost, what it means to be rejected by everybody (if they had not rejected me, why was I smothered in shame every time they looked at me?) and everything you ever thought would save you. And there were long days when I wondered why I did not die, how I could go on mindlessly living like a mule or a cow when God had obviously forsaken me. But if I was never able to accept my affliction, I was able to bear it and finally to accept the good-natured brutality and savagery in the eyes of those who came to wish me well. Mainly because of Auntie's sheer wisdom and terror. She made me see that in this world there was much more to worry about than merely being crippled.

After about a week, when it became clear that no miracle was going to save me from my bed, Willalee's grandma came up to the big house to take care of me. Getting Auntie to stay with me all of the time was the best present anyone could have given me.

All of us children, although none of us would have been able to say it, knew that Auntie was too strange—weird even—for the big people. She belonged with children, being as she was, full of the most fantastic stories and marvelous comments upon the way of the world and all things in it, whether of the earth or air. A lot of grownups had seen me by myself or with Willalee Bookatee making stories out of the Sears, Roebuck catalogue, but none of them had ever offered to join us. Not so with Auntie.

She didn't like anything better than to get right in the Sears, Roebuck catalogue with us and fix once and forever how it was between the people smiling out of the slick pages. In great detail, she told us various powers they had and about the painful curses they laid, one upon the other. She knew more about their hidden but afflicted skins than Willalee Bookatee and I had ever been able to imagine.

Somehow all of us knew that Auntie behaved as she did because she had got way beyond just being grown-up. She had grown up and up and *up* until she got to the very top, as high as you could go. Then she started down, and having been on the downhill side of growing for such a long time, she had got right back to where we were, but with an imagination more fecund and startling than any we had ever encountered.

Late in the night, when I could not sleep for the cramps in my legs, she would sit up with me sometimes for hours, talking in her old, soft, mother's voice of a world I had never heard anybody else even hint at. She loved to talk about anything with snakes in it. And even though the ring of truth that informed her voice made my skin go to goose pimples, at the same time I somehow knew that hers was a fine invention. I listened, hardly breathing, while she told me how her lifetime preoccupation with snakes had been set early for her.

"I weren't even a yearlin gul," she would say. "I was jest a little bitty thing, big as your thumb." Long, scary pause. "An I seen him in the ditch."

I had heard the story before, but I would shiver with a

delicious horror. Because I had heard it before did not mean it held any less mystery for me.

"Jest walking along and this snake I seen in the ditch had a white man's head. It was the marsah's head on the snake in the ditch."

Auntie had been born in the time of slavery. She had told me all about it a long time ago, but it never meant very much to me. It was hard to imagine what a slave might be, and it was impossible to think of people like my daddy and mama owning people like Willalee's daddy and mama. It still is.

"The bluest eyes," she said. "An marsah had the bluest eyes and that snake with marsah's head on it had them eyes and them eyes looked at me. Stopped me right where I was walkin. One foots down an one in the air and couldn't move. That snake done struck me stone still and dumb as a rock. Couldn't even holler. And he come over to me where I was still standin with my foots in the air. What he done was he come up on me and say he hongry an says I gots to haf my vittles with him, bring'm haf ever day there in the ditch and I say I will. Say I will do anything if he jest take them blue eyes off me an let me go. He did and I did."

"Did what, Auntie?" I said. I wanted the details. Details were everything.

"I *did* go back to the house and I *did* commence to start to haf up my vittles with that snake in the ditch. I took him on out there a biscuit with a hole in it. I took him on out there some of that fried poke. I took him on out there some rice, and I took him on out there vegetables when I could. An right from the first I commenced to get sick a little, chile. Didn't know jest what, but I was feelin poorly, full of the miseries, an commenced to lose flesh off my body. So one day when my Uncle Ham was to the house, I axe if he ever heard tell of anybody or other feedin a snake."

"What did he say? What?" I asked, knowing already what he said.

"Chile, he say. It was a youngun no biggern you up the other side of Lanter and she commenced to lose flesh. She was poor folks jest like us, but her mama and daddy taken vittles from their own plate an given it to that chile, given her all the syrup on all the clabber, tryin to build up that chile where she losin that flesh. Then something passin strange happen. Youngun say she got to eat by herself. She so sick, she got to have a long time and a slow time when she eat, else her stomach she know gone come up on her. She say the only thing to do is go out behind the lot to eat. So they kept on givin that gul the best they had on the table and she keep totin it all out behind the lot where she say she can have a long time an a slow time. One day her daddy followed her on out there to the other side of the lot an he find her out there *sharin* them vittles they'd taken an given her. *Sharin with a snake.* Her daddy jest went ahead on an killed that snake." She stopped and regarded the far dark window and sucked her teeth in a contemplative, satisfied way. Then, almost as an afterthought, she turned back to me and said: "His gul was dead fore he could git her back to the house."

Her voice had gone flatter and flatter, but it was coming faster, and she moved on the hard ladder-backed chair where she sat and I moved with her in my bed at the horror of it all.

"Chile, that how I got away from that blue-eyed snake with the marsah's head. When I hern tell about that gul taken and died after her snake was kilt, I known the same thing gone happen to me I keep goin out there. God in His power and mercy taken and given me the strength to leave that snake in the ditch. I ain't been sorry, neither. Naw, naawwww, I *ain't* been sorry."

Late at night she would tell me about coachwhip snakes, snakes that could wrap themselves around your leg and whip you on the back and shoulders with their platted tails, running you until they ran you to death. Then they would eat you.

And she told me about hoop snakes, snakes that had spiked tails and could form themselves into a hoop and roll after you, up hills and down hills. When they caught you, they'd hit you with the spiky end of their tails and kill you. If the spike missed you and hit a tree instead, the tree would be dead in fifteen minutes, with all the leaves on the ground because that spiky tail held killing poison.

She especially liked to talk about joint snakes, which she sometimes called glass snakes. They were pretty and seemed to be one of the few things in her world that was not deadly. When you hit or touched a joint snake, it would break into pieces about as long as a joint of your finger. It would stay that way until you left and then join itself back together. It didn't hurt the snake to be knocked apart, and it lived forever.

Perhaps most of all, she loved to talk about her daddy, dead these many years, dead so long that she had forgotten his name, calling him at various times Mr. William or Mr. John or Mr. Henry. Of all the names, though, and there were others, she favored Mr. William. He had never been bitten by a snake even though he had walked freely among them. He could just raise up his hand and tell the snakes to lie down and they would press themselves flat against the earth.

"Git down you snakes," Mr. William would say. "An them snakes'd lie down flat like they weren't no more'n a dog. I axe him how he did that and he said he didn't know how he did that but he thought anybody could do that ifn they thought they could do that but he didn't his own self know how he did that."

In the middle of the night, when the rest of the family had gone to bed and had long since been asleep, she would talk of much more than snakes. The entire world for her was aberrant and full of shadows, but she understood the aberrations and the shadows, knew all about them and never seemed to find it strange that so little of her world was what it appeared to be. One night after I had been crippled in the bed for nearly two months, she was rubbing my legs with liniment, as had become her habit. She rubbed and kneaded the fleshless, wasted bones, talking while she worked. Suddenly, she stopped, cocked her head, and seemed to listen.

"Now them birds," she said.

"Birds," I said.

"I tol you bout them birds, chile."

"No," I said. "You ain't told me bout no birds."

"Did," she said. "Did, too."

She sometimes got terribly excited if you argued too much with her in the middle of the night. I didn't want her thrashing about, falling over the furniture, getting the house up, so I just lay there shaking my head but without ever saying no to her again.

"Youngun, you oughten to have them birds in the house," she said. "A house ain't no place for no birds. Birds need to be shot. Need it bad. A wild bird oughten to be in your hand. In your house. A house is for folks. Trees and the sky yonderway for birds. I tol you bout the birds."

Auntie was not just right in the head, and I knew it. She was, as they said in Bacon County, *that way*. You couldn't go crazy in Bacon County; you were just *that way*. She was a little, frail thing who had an amazing strength in her spidery hands. Under the voluminous skirts she always wore, her bones seemed as brittle as a bird's. She was born, she was quick to tell you, a slave. But she did not know how old she was. If you asked her, she would say, "Round about a hundret." More than once mama had told me Auntie was *that way* because of her age.

In a deliberately whining voice I knew she could accept, I said. "I wish you'd *tol* me bout the birds, Auntie."

Her head cocked again, listening. "You know a bird can go ahead on a spit like a snake," she said. "Spit jest like a snake. I know you know that."

I didn't know a bird could spit like a snake, but once she said it, it sounded marvelously, horribly right to me. After the words came out of her old shrunken mouth that had known everything and said everything, it was hard for me to imagine a bird *not* spitting like a snake. And never mind that I had no idea how a snake might spit.

"Birds spit like a snake and never hit you but in one place," she said, pausing, holding the silence like a measure while she looked at me expectantly. Then, when it was obvious I didn't know: "Right in the mouf."

She got out of the chair and came to the bed and stooped for me. She took me out of the bed like my daddy might have done, in spite of the fact that wasted as I was, I must have weighed as much or more than she did. She took me out of the room and through the long shotgun corridor running down the middle of the house to the room where the birds were kept.

At the screen door giving onto the bird room, she stopped, and we stood looking in. There was enough light from the moon falling through the two tall windows for us to see the outlines of the nests where they were built on little tree limbs nailed into position on a counter along one side of the room and see the birds themselves, grown restless now, their wings fluttering and their heads bobbing silhouetted in the moonlight.

"Look in there, youngun," she said. "Look in there and *bleve*. A bird mought take you to hell. Mought take you any-wheres at all. Me, I been grieved more than some, you up here in the house with them birds. Them spittin like snakes, lookin to hit you all up in your mouf. One hit you—an one *gone* hit you—that bird own you, own all of you. Now you look in there an *bleve*."

Her old soft voice got sharp when she demanded that I be-lieve. But she could have saved it; I'd been a righteous believer in the deadly accuracy of bird spit long before we came down the hall.

"Bird spit mix all up with your spit, and then your spit is his and he's you. You listening, chile? Listen good to ole Auntie cause I think a bird . . . a bird moughta . . . a. . . ."

She could not seem to go on and turned, still holding me against her thin, bony breast, and went back down the dark-ened hallway to the room and put me in my bed. She sat again in her chair and was quiet a long time before she could speak. I waited because I knew there was more to come and she had scared me pretty good back there in the dark with the birds moving against the moonlit windows. Her mouth moved si-lently over some words.

"I think a bird is . . . spit in you mouf, chile."

I struggled to sit up but couldn't against my drawn legs, so I was reduced to getting as far away from her as I could on the other side of the bed. I was terrified. I could hear the house through the night settling around us, making all the night noises that an old house can make, beams creaking, boards popping, all of it settling deeper into its foundation.

Then in a hushed, scared voice she described in great detail how she had seen me come down the road toward the tenant house one night late, climb the fence, and start off into the cotton field. I had been wearing, she said, my gown and I had gone out into the cotton field and walked in one great circle before finally stopping and looking up into the sky at the moon for a long, long time. She had been at the window and had seen it all, and it scared her bad because she knew right off a bird must have been at my mouth and that I was not in control of what I was doing. It had been the doings of birds.

She sat a long, still time before she finally said: "Chile, if the bird done got you, don't hex on old Auntie."

She laughed in a startled kind of way. It sounded like real craziness, but she came over and tickled me. I didn't laugh with her but lay like something dead because sleepwalking had been such a mysterious, unanswerable horror, had terrified me so profoundly that I was perfectly willing to believe that I was possessed by birds, had been guided to the field by them. She kept chuckling and clucking, but when I would not respond, she went back and sat in her chair.

"Jest two things," she said. "Don't you hex and don't you conjure on Auntie. Not on ole Auntie."

I was too afraid to look at her, but when I did find the courage after a while, she had her eyes fixed upon me, and they were no longer the eyes of the little old lady I had played with and laughed with in the pages of the Sears, Roebuck catalogue. They were the eyes now of a long-caged ancient stinking monkey, crazed with some unknowable outrage.

She said: "Won't do no good conjurin on me." She leaned forward out of her chair. "I be a conjure woman, too."

I knew even then what a conjure woman was, knew that it had to do with the bones of chickens and the stomachs of goats and hair and pins and fire and sickness and death.

When I could finally speak, I said: "Ain't no bird spit in my mouth. I may be afflicted, but I ain't no bird. Nothing in here but me."

We never spoke of it again. Several times I tried unsuccessfully to work up the nerve to do it. But I *did* let the birds out of their room the next morning. Or rather I told mama to do it.

"Turn out the birds," I said when she came in with my breakfast.

"Turn'm out?" she said.

"All of'm," I said. "Don't leave one in the house."

She did not understand, but as sick as I was she would probably have done anything to keep from upsetting me. She didn't understand, but I did. I had already learned—without knowing I'd learned it—that every single thing in the world was full of mystery and awesome power. And it was only by right ways of doing things—ritual ways—that kept any of us safe. Making stories about them was not so that we could understand them but so that we could live with them. A part of me knew that, at best, I had no right to keep flying birds in a closed room, and at the same time, another part of me knew that if there were no birds in the house, one could not spit in my mouth. It all made perfect sense to me. Fantasy might not be truth as the world counts it, but what was truth when fantasy meant survival?

CHAPTER 7

I was in the bed for six weeks with my legs drawn up, and I never expect to spend a longer six weeks in my life. The visits by the doctors became fewer and fewer, and finally, they did not come anymore. They had done all they knew to do. I think I was an embarrassment to them.

The fever was gone. There were cramps still in the middle of the night, but about all that could be done for them was to have Auntie rub my legs, which she did. The uncle who spoke in tongues came back and fell across my bed several times. Even that did not cure me.

For reasons nobody ever knew, toward the end of September my legs had loosened up a little and I was able to sit on the porch for a while every day if I wanted to. I was on the porch when the last load of cotton was hauled off to Blackshear in the back of the pickup truck, on the way to a huge open-sided warehouse where the buyers would walk among the high-stacked bales, followed by the farmers, many of them wearing new overalls and new brogans, their ancient black hats pulled low over their grim faces as they listened to the buyers tell what a year of their sweat and worry was worth.

Sam sat beside me on the porch, but he too was in a bad way. Old age had dropped on him sudden as a stone. He had lost the sight in both eyes within a period of less than a week, and he had started to bleed from his ears. The bleeding was not continuous, just a kind of spotting that left an irregular and inconstant blood spoor wherever he went.

Because my legs were loose enough to allow me to be carried about over the farm to the tobacco barn, out to sit under the oak tree, down to the abandoned barn to see my goats in the afternoon, I got to see the last catch Sam ever made before he had to be taken down behind the field and killed with a shotgun. Sam and I were taking the weak fall sun on the front porch one morning when daddy came walking up from the mule lot. He carried his left arm hooked up at the elbow, his hand held up in front of him. His hand was bloody, and blood had run down over the sleeve of his shirt.

He stopped at the edge of the porch and said: "Son, I believe I'm gone have to borry your dog. Will and me been trying to load that old brood sow and damned if she ain't bout bit my finger off here."

He took me off the porch, and Sam fell in behind us, following, as he had to do now, the sound daddy's feet made over the dry sand down to the lot where the enormous sow stood grunting and snorting in the corner of the fence. Her eyes were red, and a light white froth fringed her snout. They opened the gate for Sam and whistled him inside. Once he was in the lot with the sow, daddy spoke softly to him.

"Git'er, Sam. Sic'er."

Sam's great solid head rose and his nostrils flared and his pointed ears struck forward on his head. Once he got a fix on the sow from the sound she was making backed in the corner, he did not hesitate but charged blindly. When he and the sow collided, he took a deep hold on one of her long, thick ears, and using all his weight, managing at the same time not to get caught on the tusks curling out of her mouth, he threw and held her fast, she squealing like the end of the world. Will and daddy went in and got an ear twist and nose twist on her and, after choking Sam off, led her like a lamb into the pickup truck which had high wooden livestock sides on it.

There was a snap in the air now and the winds every day grew higher than the day before and the leaves were beginning to thin on the oak tree. By the first of October I was able to ride around the farm in my goat cart pulled by Old Black Bill. Willalee Bookatee was not allowed to ride with me but had to walk alongside the cart instead. I felt very keenly how being a cripple had ruined our play, ruined all the things we used to do. That knowledge made me miserable and bad company. If Willalee minded it, he never said anything about it as he followed my cart around the fields in early fall.

We watched them bank sweet potatoes in pyramid-shaped mounds of earth and straw in such fashion that they would keep all winter long, and we watched them take the Irish potatoes to the cotton house (which would not be used again to store cotton for nearly a year) and spread them out in a single layer over the entire floor. And when the air got sharp enough, we watched daddy castrate twenty shoats in a single morning, watched him as he stood straddle of the pigs, one foot on their heads, their legs spread and he, bloody up to his elbows, reached and made two neat delicate incisions, removed the shoats' gonads, first one, and then the other, and finally tossed them into a pan where later they would be deep-fried in a flour batter. With such skill and grace and precision did he move that the entire operation seemed a single movement.

Then the ride ended one day because mama decided it was too cold even though I was bundled up nicely there behind Old Black Bill. I felt relief as much as anything else, grateful as I was to get inside where nobody else could see me. More than one mule and wagon passing on the high road had stopped while a gaunt farmer and his wife—sometimes with a wagon bed full of children—stared at me. Looking the way I did, I knew it was inevitable that the county begin thinking of me not as a cripple but as "that way." And I desperately did not want to be *that way*.

So I had to go back to my bed, which had been moved by the fireplace in the living room. But I didn't have to stay in the bed all the time. My heels were no longer drawn up tightly against me. I could crab about over the house in surprisingly quick lateral movement.

One of my favorite places to be was in the corner of the room where the ladies were quilting. God, I loved the click of needles on thimbles, a sound that will always make me think of stories. When I was a boy, stories were conversation and conversation was stories. For me it was a time of magic.

It was always the women who scared me. The stories that

women told and that men told were full of violence, sickness, and death. But it was the women whose stories were unrelieved by humor and filled with apocalyptic vision. No matter how awful the stories were that the men told they were always funny. The men's stories were stories of character, rather than of circumstance, and they always knew the people the stories were about. But women would repeat stories about folks they did not know and had never seen, and consequently, without character counting for anything, the stories were as stark and cold as legend or myth.

It is midmorning, and the women have been sewing since right after breakfast when the light first came up. They are quilting, four women, one on each side of a square frame that has been suspended from the ceiling to hold the quilt. When they are through for the day, the frame can be drawn up to the ceiling out of the way, but for now the needles and thimbles click over the quiet, persistent drone of their voices.

I sit on the floor, and with me are two white-haired children, brightly decorated with purple medicine used for impetigo, and we sit there on the floor, the three of us, sucking on sugar tits, trying to avoid the notice of our mothers, who will only stop long enough to slap us if the noise of our play gets in the way of the necessary work of making quilts.

The sugar tits we are sucking on are to quiet and pacify us through the long day. They could not have worked better if they had been opium instead of flour soaked with syrup or sometimes plain sugar wrapped in a piece of cloth. We chew on the cloth and slowly the melting sweetness seeps onto our tongues and it puts us into a kind of stupor of delight, just the mood to receive the horror story when it comes.

"The Lord works in mysterious ways."

The needles click; the heavy, stockinged legs shift almost imperceptibly.

"None of us knows the reason."

They start talking about God. We know the horror story's coming.

"But it is a reason."

"Like the song says: Farther along we'll understand why."

"In heaven it'll all be clearer, but here on earth He works in mysterious ways His many miracles to perform."

"It's no way to understand how things can sometimes be so awful. We jest got to take the good with the bad."

"I reckon."

"A week ago tomorrow I heard tell of something that do make a body wonder, though."

Nobody asks what she heard. They know she'll tell. The needles click over the thimbles in the stretching silence. Down on the floor we stop sucking and have the sugar tits caught between our teeth.

Here it comes.

"You all member Bernice's next to youngest girl, Flo?"

"Is it the one with that pretty yeller hair saved at Ten Mile Baptist Church when Reverend Harvey was in to preach?"

"That's the one, always smart as a whip and they sent her to Waycross, all the way there, after graduation to college, took a business course and she's been working with Dr. Barnes in Almer since she had to quit school when that youngest of theirs was born. Anyway, I was over there a week ago tomorrow when Flo come in from work—got a real good job answering the telephone and typing up things. She took the typewriter in college, you know. She come on in from work and told me and Bernice the whole thing."

She stopped to draw a long good breath, and the clicking needles hesitate while the breath is drawn and then click furiously, faster than ever.

"A womern come in off the street and set down. Flo didn't know her but thought she might could have been a Woodbine womern, course it could a been any of'm at all or somebody else from down in there. Dr. Barnes, you know, done a lot of charity in Woodbine. Didn't give her name to Flo, that is one of Flo's jobs to git their names, but the womern didn't give it or nothing, jest set down there and Flo seen blood running down her laig.

"Said the womern looked in her face like she was asleep or something, not crying or moaning, and all the time blood—an I don't mean a little blood but I mean blood everywhere—was puddling in the floor like you'd taken and cut a hog's throat and it was coming from under this woman's dress and a running down her laig."

And us there on the floor thinking, Merciful God, we'll all drown in blood before this is over.

"Flo didn't do a thing but go back there and tell Dr. Barnes it was a womern out there a setting in the chair a bleeding. Course, Dr. Barnes, he went right and got her and tuck her in his little room and it weren't but a minute before Flo said she heard screaming and she known right off what it was and she run back there and opened the door to that little room. It was then that she seen it."

Under the frame we can see all movement leave the stockinged legs, the knees tense, flex—all except the legs of the woman telling the story. Hers move in a timely, monotonous rhythm with the sound of her voice. And then the voice stopped, I remember her legs never missing a beat in the curious little dance she is doing.

"What Flo seen was the doctor had bent the womern over a table and had her dress flung up over her head and from between. . . ."

Here a nervous glance at us, sitting rigid now against the wall, our teeth caught in the sugar tits in a spasm of horror.

". . . between her cheeks—and I'm talking about the aner— out of her very aner came this little arm with a little hand on the end of it.

"It was a little baby arm. Flo said she couldn't breathe, talk, or do nothing but just stand there staring at that little arm with that little hand on the end of it. Flo said them little fingers commenced to move, wrinkled as prunes, and them little fingers seemed like they was a beckoning at Flo. Them's her very words: *a beckoning*.

"Flo said she felt like she was gone faint, but before she could do it, the doctor took hold of that little arm, and when he did, that womern taken and given another scream and jumped from where he had her flung over the table and run out of the room. Flo almost fainted, she said, but she didn't till she saw how it all come out. The doctor run after her and it taken three men to catch her in the street and hold her while the doctor taken and given her a shot."

Down on the floor I would have sucked all the sweetness out of the sugar tit and by then eaten most of the sacking that held it.

At night it was a different story. Since I had become sick, we had a lot of company, especially at night. The people in the county had never seen such legs as mine. The first thing they had to do was inspect my legs, staring at me where I lay, often wanting to touch me, sometimes actually doing it, ten or twelve people in a row.

Then some of them would leave and some would stay to sit by the fireplace late into the night, listening to the men talk, staying so late now and then they would end up staying all night, particularly if it was a weekend.

Because the only fireplace was in the living room where I lay, everybody gathered there after supper to watch the fire and eventually wash their feet and go off to bed. If it was a very cold night, they would carry a heated quilt from the fire to put over the icy sheets.

The stories start early in the night when the fire is as big as the hearth will hold, making its own sucking roar counterpoint to the roar of the wind under the shingled eaves of the house. Men and women and children sit in a wide semicircle, faces cast red and hollow-eyed by the fire. Auntie, who still stayed with me at night, floats into and out of the room, sometimes settling by my bed, sometimes going back to the kitchen to get something for me. Now and again, a woman or young girl will rise from her chair, back up to the hearthstone and discreetly lift her skirt from behind to receive the fire. My legs have loosened now to the point where I could, if I really tried, sit in a chair, and the doctors have begun to revise their original opinion and say that, yes, there was a real chance that I might walk again.

The galvanized foot tub, holding perhaps two and a half gallons of water, captures the light on its dull surface. It is sitting in front of the first man in the semicircle. The water is getting hot. At some time during the evening, the man in front of whom it sits will slip his feet into the tub and wash. Then he will slide it to the person sitting next to him, maybe a woman, or a young girl, and that person will wash.

While the men talk, the tub makes its way around the line of people warming from the fire. After the last person washes his feet, it is only minutes before the other children will have to go off to bed and leave their daddies and uncles and older brothers to sit and talk late into the night. But I, safely in my fireroom bed, am privileged to hear whatever is said.

"Well, he was always like that."

"Had to happen like it had to happen."

"He jest had to win."

"He *would* win."

"Kill him to lose, jest kill'm is all."

"I remember. . . ."

Here the man would lean back and chew on a kitchen match, and the skin would draw tight around his eyes. He might not say anything for several minutes, but those of us sitting there, watching him chew on the match stick, didn't care how long he took to start the story because we knew that he was about to make what had been only gossip before personal and immediate now. The magic words had been spoken: "I remember. . . ."

"I remember the day it happened. I wasn't sitting more than five or six feet from them when they got started talking on it. But I guess it was meant to happen. Both of them doing the same kind of work and him being like he was, it was bound to come to blood sooner or later.

"The hell of it was they liked each other. Nearabout like brothers as two people who ain't blood likely to git. It's how come them both to git on the same job at the same time climbing and topping trees for the REA right-of-way. They was both good at it, too. Jest about the god-awfulest climbers you ever seen. Like monkeys nearabout where climbing was concerned.

"First time I notice them talking about it, they was eating out of their dinner buckets, and I heard Leroy say, 'You cain't beat me at nothing. That's what you can beat me at, Pete, *nothing*.'

"What they was arguing about was which one of them could climb the fastest, and Leroy, of course, right away said it was him, said there was nobody in the state of Georgia could climb a tree or nothing else as fast as him, Leroy, could. Leroy's face was all red, the veins standing out in his neck, and he was kind of slobbering like a dog. You remember, he was bad to slobber. Oh, he was hot about it, he was.

"Pete musta said he could climb faster than Leroy—I didn't hear it, but that musta been what he said—and now Leroy was inviting him out to see which one of them was the best at it. You see, we'd put up light poles down the middle of the right-of-way we'd cut, but it weren't no insulation knobs or cross-pieces on them yetawhile.

"Nothing wouldn't do Leroy, soon as Pete said he could climb faster'n him, but the two of'm go on out there and both of'm git at the bottom of two different poles and somebody else git between the two poles to start'm climbing by clapping his hands. First one to the top could be the winner. Leroy wouldn't have it no other way.

"Pete tried to back out of it three times, but Leroy said: 'No, goddammit, you ought not to a gone and said I couldn't do it. Said I was slower'n you. Now we got to see whose ass is the blackest.'

"That boy had a bad mouth, he did. Always had one, jest like his daddy. Anyway, they got up from their dinner buckets and put on their climbing rigs: big thick safety belts that loop around the pole, then inch-and-a-half climbing jack-spikes buckled to their boots. Leroy walked off down the line and got at the bottom of one of them lectric poles and Pete, he got on the Nigh pole. On account of I was the closest one to him, they said: 'You get in the middle there, Bob, and do it for us. You clap the third time, we go.'

"Well, I didn't want to do it cause I was afraid Pete might somehow beat him, and if he did, Leroy might kill somebody, maybe hisself. He was crazy about winning. At anything. I'd heard him myself say he'd jest as soon die as lose. Nothing wouldn't do him, though, but I git in the middle and start them off, which I did.

"They had the wide safety belts looped around the poles and their spikes set when I clapped my hand. They started climbing, and I seen right away that Leroy didn't have nothing to worry about. It made me feel better that nobody was gone git hurt, and I stood back to watch the climb.

"Before his spikes hit the pole six times, he was already a foot higher than Pete was. What he was doing, see, was going for it, gonna win or bust.

"He was holding onto the safety belt that went around the pole with both hands and he was a climbing, puffing, his feet working, hitting that lectric pole with them spikes, driving up it, and when his feet would come up to take a fresh hold, he'd flip that leather belt with both hands and he was looking down, straight down between his pumping knees, and never looking up and flipping that belt and driving with his feet, and when he got to the top of the pole, well, bless Pat, he didn't do a thing but flip that leather belt right over the top of that pole and come sailing back down on the back of his head and broke his neck. Dead fore we could git there. Damn boy'd do anything to win. It was so smooth, it looked like a goddamn trick. It mighta been, too."

CHAPTER 8

Gradually, very gradually, I got more and more use of my legs, and finally, they were completely straight. I could straighten them all the way out so that the knees locked. My bed was taken out of the fireroom, and I myself was put out by the fence to hold onto the wire and walk around the house and around the house, despite the fact that from hip to heel my legs were nothing but bone loosely covered with dimpled, wrinkled skin, so ugly that nobody short of your God or your mama could have any faith in them.

I did not particularly want to walk around the house holding onto the fence. It was painful and boring and more than a little hopeless, but mama gently encouraged me and would sometimes walk along with me. If she wasn't with me, Willalee and blind Sam was nosing at my heels out there by the fence. Willalee was as depressed by my legs as I was. My being crippled had changed his life nearly as much as it had changed mine. And Sam was sick in a way he had never been before. The bleeding in his ears was not as bad as it had been, but he had started losing his teeth. Within a month of the time he had lost the first one, nearly all of them were gone. With our loving him as we all did, it was getting very close to the place where it would be unbearable.

One day Willalee's daddy, Will, came to me out by the fence. I knew right off it was going to be bad when he took my arm and helped me to the porch. Then he sent his boy home while he talked to me.

"Your daddy sent me to talk to you," he said.

"What about?"

"He woulda come hisself, but he wanted me to do hit. He thought I better do the talking."

"Do what?" I said, but I already knew. I'd known it was coming and that it wouldn't be long.

He looked out at the brown, cut-over fields under a lowering fall sky. The stalks had been cut already, cotton stalks and corn stalks and tobacco stalks, and the landscape had that butchered quality peculiar to Bacon County just before winter comes down in earnest.

"I got to take Sam off yonder behind the field," he finally said.

I didn't say anything.

"I got to do hit today." Then after a long pause: "Now."

"I reckon," I finally said.

"It ain't right to leave him like this," he said. "Sam been too good a dog. Him blind, he won't even know about hit."

"I don't reckon," I said. I was trying to keep from crying, not because Will was there, but because I felt how useless and silly it was to cry. If you couldn't cure an animal, you killed it. And nobody ever cured anything of old age. If constant and unrelievable pain was the alternative, death was right. There wasn't anything to talk about.

I could feel Sam breathing there where he stood in the dust by the porch. I didn't call his name, and I didn't look at him.

"All right," I said.

Will took a short lead rope out of his back pocket and dropped a loop around Sam's neck. Sam followed him off down the lane, his huge square head down, his wet tongue hanging out of the side of his mouth.

Later, when I was back by the fence, walking, I heard the single shotgun blast in the woods behind the house. That was when I cried.

By late January I was able to walk all the way out to the lot by myself and watch them as they sheared the mules with hand clippers. The mules would grow a thick coat of hair as winter came on to keep them warm. But when the farmers started breaking ground in early February, or as soon as the ground thawed, the mules carried so much hair that they couldn't stand to work in front of a turnplow all day unless they were clipped.

I never knew any mules that liked to have their hair cut. That busy steel mouth chewing away over their hides brought them to the place of blasted nerves and blasted bowels. The problem was solved by putting on a nose twist, a simple loop of plowline over the mule's upper lip with a stick through the loop so that it could be twisted tight enough to bring a little blood, not much, but a little blood down from the upper lip, tracing a thin line over the gum and teeth.

When the blood began to show, I began to cry. At first it was only a whimper with a few tears, but before Will, who held the twist, and daddy, who did the clipping, had finished with the third mule, I was nearly in hysterics. It embarrassed me terribly and embarrassed Willalee, too, who was there with me in the corner of the lot, but I could not help it. I do not know whether it was from my long stay in the bed with paralysis or whether it was from the increasing violence in the house at night—the shouting and screaming and sounds of breaking dishes and splintering chairs—brought on by daddy's bouts with whiskey, but I had been crying more and more as the winter deepened, crying as I had never done before, over anything or nothing. Sometimes when I was right by myself, tears would burst from my eyes.

Daddy tried to get me to go to the house, but I would not, and because I had been so sick for so long, he did not make me get out of the lot, as he might otherwise have done. They put off clipping the fourth, and last, mule until a time when they could do it without me being aware of it. And still I cried. Every time I looked up and saw the three trembling, naked mules, a bloody foam at their mouths, I fell into a louder fit of crying.

Daddy, who had been holding me in his arms, trying to comfort me, finally asked in a desperate voice—for he could not bear my tears—how I would like to go in the wagon with Will to Mr. John Turner's farm, a place about six miles away. Willalee could go, too. Since I almost never got off the farm, and had not been anywhere since I got sick, not even to church, I snuffled and hiccuped and was finally quiet.

When mama found out about it, she was immediately against it, which threw me instantly back into hysterics, and she relented. We left the farm, Willalee and I, in the bed of the wagon, wrapped up together with just our heads showing, and Will up front on the crossboard, driving the only mule on the place that still had his hair.

Will was on his way to Mr. John Turner's place to help a horsing mare couple with a jack. Will was known throughout the county as a man successful in such matters, a man who could, with his hands and voice, gentle down jacks and mares and, consequently, keep their breeding from being any bloodier than it had to be.

When we got to Mr. Turner's lot, Willalee and I climbed up on the top board of the fence and watched the mare loping around the lot, agitated, her wild eyes rolling, her tail lifted, and her jaws working around a light froth that bubbled from her mouth. We did not have to be told that she was horsing, that is to say, that she was ready to receive a male, either a stallion or a jack. From a stallion, Mr. Turner could expect a horse or mare colt in the spring; from a jack—a male donkey— he could expect a mule. In this instance, he was looking for a mule, and the jack was already there, haltered and hitched, waiting outside the lot. The jack was about half as tall as the mare, and no more than a third her weight, but he had already smelled her and his huge ears were pitched forward and his mouth, too, was champing and foaming. He was ready to work.

Will went in the lot and got a loop of plowline around the neck of the charging mare, and then a halter. While she rolled her eyes and grunted and slobbered—all the while pulling Will around the lot, dust swirling at their feet—Will talked to her in a low, unhurried voice. They let the jack in, and without hesitation he galloped across the lot on his stubby, ugly little legs and bit the mare on the rump. She, just as quickly, kicked him twice in the chest. The jack's eyes shot with blood, and he wheeled and kicked her in the side with both feet. As they pitched and rared and bit and kicked, Will—still talking on in his soft and soothing voice—was working the mare to the hole dug in the middle of the lot. He had to get the mare backed down into the hole or the little jack would never be able to mount.

On the lot fence, I had begun to whimper, not as badly as I had done earlier at the clipping, but tears were beginning to form nonetheless. There was obviously no reason to cry because nobody was doing anything to the animals; they were doing whatever hurt was being done to each other. But still the tears were about to come.

"You know how come it is," said Willalee, "mules cain't do it an git little mules like goats do it and git little goats or hogs do it?"

"No," I said. I knew it was true, but I didn't know why. I had never thought to wonder.

"Well," said Willalee, "in the time of Jesus. . . ."

While his daddy got the mare into the hole to receive the jack, Willalee Bookatee told a story he'd got from Auntie about how it was a mule that had carried the beams out of which Jesus' cross was made and for that reason the mule had forever after been deprived of the joy of coupling with his own kind.

Just as the little jack was driving the mare to her knees with his final, savage thrust, Willalee was saying in his wisest voice: "It also how come mules have to work so hard at the plow, on account of what all they done in olden time. Auntie say so."

All of us grew up in Bacon County surrounded by sexual couplings of every kind. Nobody ever tried to keep such matters from us. It would have been impossible anyhow. Even though I was only five years old at the time, in some vague, unconscious way I knew that people must do the same thing as animals, more or less, but it had never occurred to me that *I* might be expected to try it. Therefore, it was a real jolt when my brother sidled up to me one day and said: "It's time you got yourself a little piece, boy."

I knew very well what he meant, but I resisted it. "A piece of what?" I said.

He told me.

"Naaawww," I said.

"Yep," he said with chilling finality.

I told him I did not know anything about it, nothing at all. He proceeded to tell me all about it, in much greater detail than I wanted to listen to. He told me how it was done and where I was to do it—under the house—and further that I should put the girl on top of an old dishpan that he had already thoughtfully stored under there for me.

"On a damn dishpan?" I said. When I was away from grownups, I had recently begun to see how all the curse words I knew would fit my mouth.

"Ain't nothing bettern a dishpan," he said. "Put her up on that dishpan when you lay'er down and it'll turn that thing up to you like a fried egg."

I didn't know why I wanted it turned up like a fried egg, but Hoyet said I would see how it all worked once I got started. More than that, I didn't really want to do it because I couldn't see any sense in it, but my brother clinched it for me when he said: "It always comes a time in a man's life when he's got to do it. Purvis says it's sure as death." Purvis was a boy who worked for one of our uncles, but he was already old enough to come home drunk and bloody at daylight, for which we greatly admired him. If it was good enough for Purvis, it was good enough for me. Lottie Mae was the girl.

It was cold enough to crack your eyeballs, and Lottie Mae and I were bundled up in clothing. But I worked at her shivering, buttoned-up little body as best I could and finally got her out of her clothes there where I had her under the house that sat up about two and a half feet on blocks made out of brick. We were trembling, both us naked as babies, as I struggled to get her up on the dishpan. To get her square-legged, homemade drawers off I had to promise she could play with me and Willalee in the catalogue.

She didn't know any more about it than I did, and at first she thought I wanted to see her pee. When she did begin to see what I had in mind, she thought I was crazy.

"It ain't *no* way to do that," she said. "Ain't gone *do*. Try if you wants to, but I knows it won't do."

I carefully explained to her what my brother said we should do, and while I talked, I watched her eyes grow rounder and rounder and her mouth go slack, and even though she shook her head the whole time I was saying it, she did not balk at the dishpan and I finally had her on it, both of us full of chill bumps from the cold. Just as I was about to mount, to do God knows what, because in the wind I was rapidly forgetting my brother's instructions, I heard something behind me, and when I looked over my shoulder, I saw mama's stout legs, those knees flexed and ready.

"Come out from under there, youngun," mama said. And I did. I came out quickly, head already contritely down heading for the place where she would catch and hold me while she violently shredded a peach tree switch over my upturned bottom, stung by the cold, cheeks red already.

Never a word about my crippled legs and never a word about the months in bed, so recent I still had small sores the size of fever blisters on my back. It was the first whipping I'd had since I got sick, and I knew that I was well and whole again.

CHAPTER 9

As winter grew deeper and we waited for hog-killing time, at home the center was not holding. Whether it was because the crops were in and not much work was to be done or whether it was because of my having just spent so long a time crippled in the bed, daddy had grown progressively crazier, more violent. He was gone from home for longer and longer periods of time, and during those brief intervals when he was home, the crashing noise of breaking things was everywhere about us. Daddy had also taken to picking up the shotgun and screaming threats while he waved it about, but at that time he had not as yet fired it.

While that was going on, it occurred to me for the first time that being alive was like being awake in a nightmare.

I remember saying aloud to myself: "Scary as a nightmare. Jest like being awake in a nightmare."

Never once did I ever think that my life was not just like everybody else's, that my fears and uncertainties were not universal. For which I can only thank God. Thinking so could only have made it more bearable.

My sleepwalking had become worse now that I could get out of bed on my unsure legs. I woke up sometimes in the middle of the night in the dirt lane by the house or sometimes sitting in my room in a corner chewing on something. It didn't matter much what: the sleeve of my gown or the side of my hand or even one time the laces of a shoe. And when I would wake up, it was always in terror, habitually remembering now what Auntie had said about the birds spitting in my mouth. No, more than *remembering* what she had said. Rather, seeing what she had said, the image of a bird burned clearly on the backs of my eyelids, its beak hooked like the nose of a Byzantine Christ, shooting spit thick as phlegm on a solid line into my open and willing mouth. With such dreams turning in my head it came time for us to all help kill and butcher hogs. Daddy was laid up somewhere drunk; we had not seen him in four days. So he did not go with us to Uncle Alton's to help with the slaughter. Farm families swapped labor at hog-killing time just as they swapped labor to put in tobacco or pick cotton. Early one morning our tenant farmers, mama, my brother, and I walked the half mile to Uncle Alton's place to help put a year's worth of meat in the smokehouse. Later his family would come and help us do the same thing.

Before it was over, everything on the hog would have been used. The lights (lungs) and liver—together called haslet—would be made into a fresh stew by first pouring and pouring again fresh water through the slit throat—the exposed throat called a goozle—to clean the lights out good. Then the fat would be trimmed off and put with the fat trimmed from the guts to cook crisp into cracklins to mix with cornbread or else put in a wash pot to make soap.

The guts would be washed and then turned and washed again. Many times. After the guts had been covered with salt overnight, they were used as casings for sausage made from shoulder meat, tenderloin, and—if times were hard—any kind of scrap that was not entirely fat.

The eyes would be removed from the head, then the end of the snout cut off, and the whole thing boiled until the teeth could be picked out. Whatever meat was left, cheeks, ears, and so on, would be picked off, crushed with herbs and spices and packed tightly into muslin cloth for hog's headcheese.

The fat from the liver, lungs, guts, or wherever was cooked until it was as crisp as it would get and then packed into tin syrup buckets to be ground up later for cracklin cornbread. Even the feet were removed, and after the outer layer of split hooves was taken off, the whole thing was boiled and pickled in vinegar and peppers. If later in the year the cracklins started to get rank, they would be thrown into a cast-iron wash pot with fried meat's grease, any meat for that matter that might have gone bad in the smokehouse, and some potash and lye and cooked into soap, always made on the full of the moon so it wouldn't shrink. I remember one time mama out in the backyard making soap when a chicken for some reason tried to fly over the wash pot but didn't make it. The chicken dropped flapping and squawking into the boiling fat and lye. Mama, who was stirring the mixture with an old ax handle, never missed a beat. She just stirred the chicken right on down to the bottom. Any kind of meat was good for making soap.

By the time we got to Uncle Alton's the dirt floor of the smokehouse had been covered with green pine tops. After the pork stayed overnight in tubs of salt, it would be laid on the green pine straw all night, sometimes for two nights, to get all the water out of it. Then it was taken up and packed again in salt for three or four days. When it was taken out of the salt for the last time, it was dipped in plain hot water or else in a solution of crushed hot peppers and syrup or wild honey. Then it was hung over a deep pile of smoldering hickory spread across the entire floor of the smokehouse. The hickory was watched very carefully to keep any sort of blaze from flaring up. Day and night until it was over, light gray smoke boiled continuously from under the eaves and around the door where the meat was being cured. It was the sweetest smoke a man was ever to smell.

It was a bright cold day in February 1941, so cold the ground was still frozen at ten o'clock in the morning. The air was full of the steaming smell of excrement and the oily, flatulent odor of intestines and the heavy sweetness of blood—in every way a perfect day to slaughter animals. I watched the hogs called to the feeding trough just as they were every morning except this morning it was to receive the ax instead of slop.

A little slop *was* poured into their long communal trough, enough to make them stand still while Uncle Alton or his boy Theron went quietly among them with the ax, using the flat end like a sledgehammer (shells were expensive enough to make a gun out of the question). He would approach the hog from the rear while it slopped at the trough, and then he would straddle it, one leg on each side, patiently waiting for the hog to raise its snout from the slop to take a breath, showing as it did the wide bristled bone between its ears to the ax.

It never took but one blow, delivered expertly and with consummate skill, and the hog was dead. He then moved with his hammer to the next hog and straddled it. None of the hogs ever seemed to mind that their companions were dropping dead all around them but continued in a single-minded passion to eat. They didn't even mind when another of my cousins (this could be a boy of only eight or nine because it took neither strength nor skill) came right behind the hammer and drew a long razor-boned butcher knife across the throat of the fallen hog. Blood spurted with the still-beating heart, and a live hog would sometimes turn to one that was lying beside it at the trough and stick its snout into the spurting blood and drink a bit just seconds before it had its own head crushed.

It was a time of great joy and celebration for the children. We played games and ran (I gimping along pretty well by then) and screamed and brought wood to the boiler and thought of that night, when we would have fresh fried pork and stew made from lungs and liver and heart in an enormous pot that covered half the stove.

The air was charged with the smell of fat being rendered in tubs in the backyard and the sharp squeals of the pigs at the troughs, squeals from pure piggishness at the slop, never from pain. Animals were killed but seldom hurt. Farmers took tremendous precautions about pain at slaughter. It is, whether or not they ever admit it when they talk, a ritual. As brutal as they sometimes are with farm animals and with themselves, no farmer would ever eat an animal he had willingly made suffer.

The heel strings were cut on each of the hog's hind legs, and a stick, called a gambreling stick, or a gallus, was inserted into the cut behind the tendon and the hog dragged to the huge cast-iron boiler, which sat in a depression dug into the ground so the hog could be slipped in and pulled out easily. The fire snapped and roared in the depression under the boiler. The fire had to be tended carefully because the water could never quite come to a boil. If the hog was dipped in boiling water, the hair would set and become impossible to take off. The ideal temperature was water you could rapidly draw your finger through three times in succession without being blistered.

Unlike cows, which are skinned, a hog is scraped. After the hog is pulled from the water, a blunt knife is drawn over the animal, and if the water has not been too hot, the hair slips off smooth as butter, leaving a white, naked, utterly beautiful pig.

To the great glee of the watching children, when the hog is slipped into the water, it defecates. The children squeal and clap their hands and make their delightfully obscene children's jokes as they watch it all.

On that morning, mama was around in the back by the smokehouse where some hogs, already scalded and scraped, were hanging in the air from their heel strings being disemboweled. Along with the other ladies she was washing out the guts, turning them inside out, cleaning them good so they could later be stuffed with ground and seasoned sausage meat.

Out in front of the house where the boiler was, I was playing pop-the-whip as best I could with my brother and several of my cousins. Pop-the-whip is a game in which everyone holds hands and runs fast and then the leader of the line turns sharply. Because he is turning through a tighter arc than the other children, the line acts as a whip with each child farther down the line having to travel through a greater space and consequently having to go faster in order to keep up. The last child in the line literally gets *popped* loose and sent flying from his playmates.

I was popped loose and sent flying into the steaming boiler of water beside a scalded, floating hog.

I remember everything about it as clearly as I remember anything that ever happened to me, except the screaming. Curiously, I cannot remember the screaming. They say I screamed all the way to town, but I cannot remember it.

What I remember is John C. Pace, a black man whose daddy was also named John C. Pace, reached right into the scalding water and pulled me out and set me on my feet and stood back to look at me. I did not fall but stood looking at John and seeing in his face that I was dead.

The children's faces, including my brother's, showed I was dead, too. And I knew it must be so because I knew where I had fallen and I felt no pain—not in that moment—and I knew with the bone-chilling certainty most people are spared that, yes, death does come and mine had just touched me.

John C. Pace ran screaming and the other children ran screaming and left me standing there by the boiler, my hair and skin and clothes steaming in the bright cold February air.

In memory I stand there alone with the knowledge of death upon me, watching steam rising from my hands and clothes while everybody runs and, after everybody has gone, standing there for minutes while nobody comes.

That is only memory. It may have been but seconds before my mama and Uncle Alton came to me. Mama tells me she heard me scream and started running toward the boiler, knowing already what had happened. She has also told me that she could not bring herself to try to do anything with that smoking ghostlike thing standing by the boiler. But she did. They all did. They did what they could.

But in that interminable time between John pulling me out and my mother arriving in front of me, I remember first the pain. It didn't begin as bad pain, but rather like maybe sandspurs under my clothes.

I reached over and touched my right hand with my left, and the whole thing came off like a wet glove. I mean, the skin on the top of the wrist and the back of my hand, along with the fingernails, all just turned loose and slid on down to the ground. I could see my fingernails lying in the little puddle my flesh made on the ground in front of me.

Then hands were on me, taking off my clothes, and the pain turned into something words cannot touch, or at least my words cannot touch. There is no way for me to talk about it because when my shirt was taken off, my back came off with it. When my overalls were pulled down, my cooked and glowing skin came down.

I still had not fallen, and I stood there participating in my own butchering. When they got the clothes off me, they did the worst thing they could have done; they wrapped me in a sheet. They did it out of panic and terror and ignorance and love.

That day there happened to be a car at the farm. I can't remember who it belonged to, but I was taken into the backseat into my mama's lap—God love the lady, out of her head, pressing her boiled son to her breast—and we started for Alma, a distance of about sixteen miles. The only thing that I can remember about the trip was that I started telling mama that I did not want to die. I started saying it and never stopped.

The car we piled into was incredibly slow. An old car and very, very slow, and every once in a while Uncle Alton, who was like a daddy to me, would jump out of the car and run alongside it and helplessly scream for it to go faster and then he would jump on the running board until he couldn't stand it any longer and then he would jump off again.

But like bad beginnings everywhere, they sometimes end well. When I got to Dr. Sharp's office in Alma and he finally managed to get me out of the sticking sheet, he found that I was scalded over two-thirds of my body but that my head had not gone under the water (he said that would have killed me), and for some strange reason I have never understood, the burns were not deep. He said I would probably even outgrow the scars, which I have. Until I was about fifteen years old, the scars were puckered and discolored on my back and right arm and legs. But now their outlines are barely visible.

The only hospital at the time was thirty miles away, and Dr. Sharp said I'd do just as well at home if they built a frame over the bed to keep the covers off me and also kept a light burning over me twenty-four hours a day. (He knew as well as we did that I couldn't go to a hospital anyway, since the only thing Dr. Sharp ever got for taking care of me was satisfaction for a job well done, if he got that. Over the years, I was his most demanding and persistent charity, which he never mentioned to me or mama. Perhaps that is why in an age when it is fashionable to distrust and hate doctors, I love them.)

So they took me back home and put a buggy frame over my
bed to make it resemble, when the sheet was on it, a covered
wagon, and ran a line in from the Rural Electrification Ad-
ministration so I could have the drying light hanging just over
me. The pain was not nearly so bad now that I had for the first
time in my life the miracle of electricity close enough to touch.
The pain was bad enough, though, but relieved to some extent
by some medicine Dr. Sharp gave us to spray out of a bottle
onto the burns by pumping a black rubber ball. When it dried,
it raised to form a protective, cooling scab. But it was bad to
crack. The bed was always full of black crumbs, which Auntie
worked continually at. When they brought me home, Auntie,
without anybody saying a word to her, came back up the road
to take care of me.

The same day Hollis Toomey came, too. He walked into the
house without knocking or speaking to anyone. Nobody had
sent for him. But whenever anybody in the county was burned,
he showed up as if by magic, because he could talk the fire out
of you. He did not call himself a faith healer, never spoke of
God, didn't even go to church, although his family did. His
was a gift that was real, and everybody in the county knew it
was real. For reasons which he never gave, because he was the
most reticent of men and never took money or anything else
for what he did, he was drawn to a bad burn the way iron fil-
ings are drawn to a magnet, never even saying, "You're welcome," to those who thanked him. He was as sure of his
powers and as implacable as God.

When he arrived, the light had not yet been brought into the
house, and the buggy frame was not yet over my bed and I was
lying in unsayable pain. His farm was not far from ours, and it
was unlike any other in the county. Birds' nests made from
gourds, shaped like crooked-necked squash with a hole cut in
one side with the seeds taken out, hung everywhere from the
forest of old and arching oak trees about his house. Undulating
flocks of white pigeons flew in and out of his hayloft. He had a
blacksmith shed, black as smut and always hot from the open
hearth where he made among other things iron rims for wagon
wheels. He could handcraft a true-shooting gun, including the

barrel which was not smooth-bore but had calibrated riflings. He owned two oxen, heavier than mules, whose harness, including the double yoke, he had made himself. His boys were never allowed to take care of them. He watered them and fed them and pulled them now and again to stumps or trees. But he also had the only Belgian draft horse in the county. The horse was so monstrously heavy that you could hitch him to two spans of good mules—four of them—and he would walk off with them as though they were goats. So the oxen were really useless. It just pleased him to keep them.

He favored very clean women and very dirty men. He thought it was the natural order of things. One of the few things I ever heard him say, and he said it looking off toward the far horizon, speaking to nobody: "A man's got the *right* to stink."

His wife always wore her hair tightly bunned at the back of her head under a stiffly starched white bonnet. Her dresses were nearly to her ankles, and they always looked and smelled as if they had just come off the clothesline after a long day in the sun.

Hollis always smelled like his pockets were full of ripe chicken guts, and his overalls were as stiff as metal. He didn't wear a beard; he wore a stubble. The stubble was coal black despite the fact he was over sixty, and it always seemed to be the same length, the length where you've got to shave or start telling everybody you're growing a beard. Hollis Toomey did neither.

When I saw him in the door, it was as though a soothing balm had touched me. This was Hollis Toomey, who was from my county, whose boys I knew, who didn't talk to God about your hurt. He didn't even talk to *you*; he talked to the *fire*. A mosquito couldn't fly through a door he was standing in he was so wide and high, and more, he was obviously indestructible. He ran on his own time, went where he needed to go. Nobody ever thought of doing anything for him, helping him. If he wanted something, he made it. If he couldn't make it, he took it. Hollis Toomey was not a kind man.

My daddy had finally come home, red-eyed and full of puke. He was at the foot of the bed, but he didn't say a word while Hollis sat beside me.

Hollis Toomey's voice was low like the quiet rasping of a file on metal. I couldn't hear most of what he had to say, but that was all right because I stopped burning before he ever started talking. He talked to the fire like an old and respected adversary, but one he had beaten consistently and had come to beat again. I don't remember him once looking at my face while he explained: "Fire, this boy is mine. This bed is mine. This room is mine. It ain't nothing here that's yours. It's a lot that is, but it ain't nothing here that is."

At some point while he talked he put his hands on me, one of them spread out big as a frying pan, and I was already as cool as spring water. But I had known I would be from the moment I had seen him standing in the door. Before it was over, he cursed the fire, calling it all kinds of sonofabitch, but the words neither surprised nor shocked me. The tone of his voice made me know that he was locked in a real and terrible conflict with the fire. His hands flexed and hurt my stomach, but it was nothing compared to the pain that had been on me before he came.

I had almost dozed off when he suddenly got up and walked out of the room. My daddy called, "Thank you," in a weak, alcohol-spattered voice. Hollis Toomey did not answer.

When they finally got the buggy frame up, it was not as terrible as I at first thought it was going to be. I was, of course, by then used to the bed and that was no problem and the buggy frame gave a new dimension, a new feeling to the sickbed. With the frame arching over me it was a time for fantasy and magic because I lived in a sort of playhouse, a kingdom that was all mine.

At least I pretended it was a kingdom, pretended it in self-defense. I did not want to be there, but there was no help for it, so I might as well pretend it was a kingdom as anything else. And like every child who owns anything, I ruled it like a tyrant. There was something very special and beautiful about being the youngest member of a family and being badly hurt.

Since it pleased me to do so, I spent a lot of time with the Sears, Roebuck catalogue, started writing and nearly finished a detective novel, although at that time I had never seen a novel, detective or otherwise. I printed it out with a soft-lead pencil on lined paper, and it was about a boy who, for his protection, carried not a pistol but firecrackers. He solved crimes and gave things to poor people and doctors. The boy was also absolutely fearless.

I was given a great deal of ginger ale to drink because the doctor or mama or somebody thought that where burns were concerned, it had miraculous therapeutic value. This ginger ale was the store-bought kind, too, not some homemade concoction but wonderfully fizzy and capped in real bottles. Since Hoyet and I almost never saw anything from the store, I drank as much of it as they brought me, and they brought me a lot. I never learned to like it but could never get over my fascination with the bubbles that rose in the bottle under the yellow light hanging from the buggy frame.

But I was tired of being alone in bed, and since I was going into my second major hurt back to back, I decided I might as well assert myself.

Old Black Bill had sired several kids the previous spring, and one of them was himself black and a male, so I named him Old Black Bill, too, and he grew up with me under the buggy frame. No animal is allowed in a farmhouse in Bacon County, at least to my knowledge. Dogs stay in the yard. Cats usually live in the barn catching rats, and goats, well, goats only get in the house if they have first been butchered for the table.

But I had been scalded and I was special. And I knew even then that an advantage unused becomes no advantage at all. So I insisted Old Black Bill's kid be brought to my bed. I was only about three weeks into my recovery, and I thought that a goat would be good company.

They brought him in, and I fed him bits of hay and shelled corn under the buggy frame. We had long conversations. Or rather, I had long monologues and he, patiently chewing, listened.

The two tall windows at the foot of my bed opened onto a forty-acre field. Through the long winter days Old Black Bill and I watched it being prepared to grow another crop. First the cornstalks were cut by a machine with revolving blades, pulled by a single mule. Then two mules were hitched to a big rake, so big a man could ride on it. When all the stalks were piled and burned, the land had to be broken, completely turned under, the single hardest job on a farm for the farmer and his mules.

Every morning, when the light came up enough for me to see into the field, Willalee's daddy, Will, would already be out there behind a span of mules walking at remarkable speed, breaking the hard, clayish earth more than a foot deep. Sometimes daddy was out there plowing, too. Most of the time he was not.

Willalee's daddy would mark off an enormous square, fifteen acres or better, then follow that square around and around, always taking about a fourteen-inch bite with the turnplow so that when he went once around on each of the four sides of the square, the land still to be broken would have been reduced by fourteen inches on a side.

A man breaking land would easily walk thirty miles or more every day, day in and day out, until the entire farm was turned under. Even though the mules were given more corn and more hay than they were used to, they still lost weight. Every night when they were brought to the barn, they had high stiff ridges of salt outlining where their collars and backbands and trace chains and even their bridles had been.

With only my head out from under the buggy frame, continually dried and scabbed by the burning light, I watched the plows drag on through the long blowing days, Willalee's daddy moving dim as a ghost in the sickly half-light of the winter sun. Then after the longest, hardest time, the turnplow was taken out of the field, and the row marker brought in to lay off the lines in the soft earth where the corn would finally begin to show in the springtime. The row marker was made out of a trunk of a tree, sometimes a young oak, more often a pine, made by boring holes thirty-six inches apart and inserting a straight section of limb into each of the holes. Two holes were bored into the top of the log for handles and two holes in the front of the log for the shaves, between which the mule was hitched to drag the whole rig across the turned-under field, marking off four rows at a time.

Some farmers always had crops that grew in rows straight as a plumb line. Others didn't seem to care about it much, one way or the other. It was not unusual for a farmer bumping along in a wagon behind a steaming mule in the heat of summer to comment on how the rows were marked off on each farm he passed.

"Sumbitch, he musta been drunk when he laid them off."

"I bet he has to git drunk again ever time he plows that mess."

"I guess he figgers as much'll grow in a crooked row as a straight one."

For reasons I never knew, perhaps it was nothing more complicated than pride of workmanship, farmers always associated crooked rows with sorry people. So much of farming was beyond a man's control, but at least he could have whatever nature allowed to grow laid off in straight rows. And the feeling was that a man who didn't care enough to keep his rows from being crooked couldn't be much of a man.

In all the years in Bacon County, I never saw any rows straighter than the ones Willalee's daddy put down. He would take some point of reference at the other end of the field, say, a tree or a post, and then keep his eye on it as the mule dragged the row marker over the freshly broken ground, laying down those first critical rows. If the first four rows were straight, the rest of the field would be laid off straight, because the outside marker would always run in the last row laid down.

It didn't hurt to have a good mule. As was true of so many other things done on the farm, it was much easier if the abiding genius of a good mule was brought to bear on the job. There were mules in Bacon County that a blind man could have laid off straight rows behind. Such mules knew only one way to work: the right way. To whatever work they were asked to do, they brought a lovely exactitude, whether it was walking off rows, snaking logs, sledding tobacco without a driver, or any of the other unaccountable jobs that came their way during a crop year.

After the field was marked in a pattern of rows, Willalee's daddy came in with the middlebuster, a plow with a wing on both sides that opens up the row to receive first the fertilizer and then the seed. When all the rows had been plowed into shallow trenches, Will appeared in the field early one morning with a two-horse wagon full of guano, universally called *gyou-anner.* It was a commercial fertilizer sold in 200-pound bags, and Will had loaded the wagon before daylight by himself and brought it at sunup into the field where he unloaded one bag every three rows across the middle of the field.

Shortly after he left with the wagon, he came back with the guano strower and Willalee Bookatee. Willalee had a tin bucket with him. He plodded sleepily behind his daddy, the bucket banging at his knees. The guano strower was a kind of square wooden box that got smaller at the bottom, where there was a metal shaft shaped like a corkscrew and over which the guano had to fall as it poured into the trench opened by the middlebuster. The corkscrew shaft broke up any lumps in the fertilizer and made sure it kept flowing. Two little tongue-shaped metal plows at the back of the guano strower were set so that one ran on each side of the furrow. They covered up the thin stream of fertilizer the instant after it was laid down.

Willalee was out there to fill up the guano strower for his daddy, a bad, boring job and one reserved exclusively for small boys. Willalee would open one of the bags, fill the strower, and his daddy would head for the end of the row. As soon as he was gone, Willalee would go back to the sack, and since he could not pick up anything that heavy, he would have to dip the bucket full with his hands. Then he had nothing to do but shift from foot to foot, the fertilizer burning his arms and hands and before long his eyes, and wait for his daddy to come back down the row. When he did, Willalee would fill up the strower and the whole thing would be to do over again.

CHAPTER 10

By the time the field was covered with corn about an inch high I was able to do without the buggy frame and the constantly burning light. Dr. Sharp also said I could stay out of bed all I wanted to if the pain was not too bad.

Then two things happened in the same day: I saw my first grapefruit, and daddy went briefly crazy. I always remember the two things together. They got mixed and twisted in such a way that in the months to come, my nose would sometimes fill with the oily, biting smell of grapefruit.

My brother was going to the schoolhouse a half mile away on the same dirt road as our farm, and every other Thursday the federal government sent out a big truck filled with food of one kind or another, mostly in cans, for the children to take home.

"What all was it in the commodities truck?" I asked immediately upon seeing my brother's face when he came home from school.

"It was everything it ever was. And something else besides, too."

Mama had come in the room where we were. She stood wiping her hands on her apron.

"Did you git your commodity?" I asked, knowing he would never have come gloating into my room like that if he had not. But I'd really asked just so I could say the word *commodity*. All of us loved the word and put some pretty good mileage on it every other Thursday during the school year. I didn't have the slightest notion of what *commodity* meant. To me it meant: free food that comes on a truck. I've since managed to find the several definitions of the word, but in my secret heart I'll always know what commodity means: *free food that comes on a truck*.

"What did you git, son?" mama asked.

"Oh, I got my commodity," Hoyet said, drawing the whole thing out for as long as he could.

"You lost it. You lost your damn commodity," I said in a choked, accusing voice, hoping that saying he'd lost it would make him produce it. Which he did. While mama scowled and warned me about cursing—a habit I'd developed with some vigor because my nearly mortal hurts made everybody spoil me, even mama—my brother whipped his hand from behind his back.

"Godamighty," I said. "Is it a orange or just what?"

"That commodity right there," said my brother in a voice suddenly serious as death, "is a grapefruit."

The words *grape* and *fruit* did not seem to me to cover it. We all stood silently staring at the round golden thing in his hand, so strange there in the tag end of winter, when everything in Bacon County was burned brown with cold and broken in the field. Then I began to smell it, *really* smell it, a smell full of the sun and green leaves and a sweet tongue and a delightfully cool bellyful of juice.

"See," he said. "We could have a can of Campbell's pork and beans or one of these."

"And you took this," I said.

"It don't look like pork and beans, do it?" he said. Then: "It's just like a orange, only bigger."

We knew all about oranges, or not all about them, but we did see them from time to time, little, shriveled, discolored things. But this was orange to the tenth power, which was precisely the way we thought about it even though obviously we could not have said it.

We all smelled it, pressing it against our noses, and felt it and held it longer than was necessary. Mama had brought the butcher knife from the kitchen.

"You reckon we ought to wait for daddy?" I said, a genuinely optimistic question since we hadn't seen him in almost a week.

"Ain't no use to wait," Hoyet said. His expression did not change. He raised the plump grapefruit to his face and peeled it back. Then we halved it and lifted off carefully and deliberately one slice at a time. The slices, which we called slisures, were dripping and yellow as flowers.

But I only had to touch my lips to my piece to know that something was wrong, bad wrong. "Damn if I don't believe my slisure's ruint," I said.

"Do taste a little rank, don't it?" Hoyet said.

Mama made me come over to her so she could hit me. She said: "Come over here so I can slap your head, boy. You cain't talk like that in my house." She liked to make you come to her to get your lick sometimes because she knew the humiliation made it worse. Soon as she had my head ringing like a bell tower she gently and sadly explained the bitter truth about certain grapefruit. "But they tell me," she said, "grapefruits is real good for you. Howsomever, to me they do taste a lot like a green persimmon."

We stood there in the room and gagged down that whole sour thing, slice by slice. It wouldn't do to let a commodity go to waste. The federal government had hauled it all the way to the schoolhouse, and Hoyet had deliberately chosen it over pork and beans and then brought it home in the empty syrup bucket with the wire bale on top he used to carry his lunch to school. That was why it had to be eaten, as mama carefully explained, while we chewed and swallowed, swallowed and chewed.

Finally, it was over. All that remained were a few seeds, a little pulp, and the skin. As soon as I could do it without either of them knowing, I went outside, leaned over the fence, and threw up. When I finally raised my head, I saw Willalee. His back was to me, down in the dirt lane by his house, too far to call him. It was the last time I ever saw him because that night daddy shot the mantelshelf off the fireplace with a twelve-gauge shotgun.

I heard the pickup truck and heard him when he came in and knew without thinking it was going to be a bad night. For about an hour, things were bad in the way they had been bad before: incredibly imaginative cursing between mama and daddy delivered at the top of their voices; pots and pans bouncing off the walls of the kitchen, where daddy had gone to feed the long bout he'd had with whiskey; dishes breaking; the dull unmistakable thump of flesh on flesh. The old house was shaking and I was shaking and my brother, who had started sleeping in the same bed with me again now that my burn had pretty much healed, my brother was shaking too.

Then the shotgun, the eye-rattling blast of a twelve-gauge, so unthinkably loud that it blew every other sound out of the house, leaving a silence scarier than all the noise that preceded it. The sound we had all waited for and expected for so long had finally come. It literally shattered our lives in fact and in memory.

We left in the dead of night, mama, my brother, and I, daddy behind us, silhouetted by the kerosene lamp and raving in the doorway. It had all happened quickly in confusion and fear, all of us rushing through the smell of gunpowder, putting something—I don't remember what—in a little pasteboard box for my brother to carry. Mama jerking me into my overalls and tying the string on a tiny straw suitcase at the same time.

Daddy had followed us about the house, alternately begging mama to stay and threatening to shoot something else if she did. There was no doubt in my mind that what he might shoot was me or all of us. But I still loved him. For all I knew, every family was like that. I knew for certain it was not unusual for a man to shoot at his wife. It was only unusual if he hit her. I had heard enough stories—many of them told by the same wife the shot had barely missed—to know that.

But this was the first time daddy ever fired the gun in the house, and certainly it was the first time mama—her face utterly pale except for her blue lips—had bundled us out in a chilly, moonless night to walk the half mile to Uncle Alton's house. My brother and I tried a few questions on the way, timid, unsure questions that brought no answer. My scalded legs were not hurting, but I was scared and unable to stop

crying, so I said they were. I stumbled along in the deep ruts
behind mama, following her in the dark by the sound of her
strained, constricted breathing. In one long, strangled sob I
told her that all my burns hurt and that my infantile paralysis
hurt and that I wished I could go back home.

She never slowed or broke her stride, and I could tell by the
muffled quality of her voice that she didn't even turn her head
to look back at me when she said: "Wish in one hand and shit
in the other. See which one fills up first."

It was not like mama to talk like that to a youngun exposed
to the night air, and I knew once and forever that nothing in
our lives would ever be as it had been again. So right there in
the road, unable to see my hand in front of my face, I came
apart a little more. The seams began to fray and unravel along
all my joinings. Further, something that had never happened
before, I began to feel myself as a slick, bloodless picture looking up from a page, dressed so that all my flaws whatsoever
but particularly my malformed bones were cleverly hidden.

I knew that it was not true, that it was made up, and that
also it was a kind of cheating to go about pretending you were
what you were not. But there seemed to be no alternative. It
only needed to be done with enough conviction to keep from
going crazy. The only way to deal with the real world was to
challenge it with one of your own making. For a long time
after that, the next six months, from March to August, lived
in my memory as a series of scenes, flashes of actions lit down
to the most brutal detail under a blinding light.

We stood in the lane, not going near the yard gate while two
cowering hounds bayed at us from under the front door step.
Finally, we saw the flare of a match and then the steady light
of a kerosene lamp. Uncle Alton, only one strap of his overalls
gallus strapped over his longjohns, stood in the door with the
lamp held high as he called to the hounds.

Mama marched across the yard and up the steps, stopping
inches from Uncle Alton. Her face was turned up under the
high-held light, showing her blue, unreal mouth. And when
her lips moved, it was as though they were controlled by

nothing so subtle as a mind but instead by something mechanical and arbitrarily calibrated like the strings of a puppeteer.

When finally she did speak, her voice held hate enough to break the backs of all the peoples of the world. "If I'd a been six inches taller, you'd be talking to my ghost. He taken the gun and shot the mantelshelf."

The next day in the afternoon we left Bacon County— packed onto the bus with two old suitcases and some stuff tied up with string and a shoebox full of chicken and biscuit on the road to Jacksonville, Florida, 100 miles away. I had not heard of Hitler's cattle cars then, but when I think of that trip, I remember it most often in that image. Tired people savaged by long years of scratching in soil already worn out before they were born. There was no talk in the crowded hot bus. When we had to slow down for traffic or for one of the little towns along the way where everything looked temporary, as though it might all be taken down during the night and hauled away, the greasy odor of burned fuel floated in through the open windows, choking us where we sat. But even on the straightaway, driving steadily between stunted forests of second-growth pine, an unbreathable, malodorous fog of combustion seeped up through the paneling at the bottom of the bus. Babies and little children moaned in their sleep when they breathed it.

Mama reached over and shook me gently where I sat by the window. "Wake up and look at that," she said. "It's the border keeping Georgia and Florida separate."

But I had not been asleep. I'd just had my forehead pressed against the window, which was not cool, but it was not as hot as everything else. It was after sundown, but there was plenty of light to see the river, and when mama touched me, I was already staring at its black surface, wondering what it would be like to fish from one of the little black boats I could see as the bus hurtled over the bridge, and wondering, too, about the marvel of the river, long and slow and snaky, pouring between banks of oak and black gum and sometimes cypress, pouring under bridges and on past little towns and maybe big ones—*all the time keeping everything that was Georgia away from everything that was Florida.*

It was a magic moment for me because I had always been fascinated with boundaries and borders—the Little Satilla, for instance, separating Appling County from Bacon, made me feel safe and good when I started to sleep at night, knowing that it was keeping all of us in and all of them out—but the St. Marys River was a border that went beyond fascination. Before mama spoke to me, I had recognized the river although I had never seen it before. I knew also it formed the border although I don't remember anybody ever telling me that it did. The vague shapes of streets and houses and buildings and factories began to filter down behind my eyes. I knew I had never seen any of it before, but if I concentrated, I could see all of it.

Still seeing the streets and buildings I had never seen before, I suddenly shocked myself by saying: "We gone go right on over to the Springfield Section."

I knew absolutely, without knowing how I knew it, that something called the Springfield Section of Jacksonville was where all of us from Bacon County went, when we had to go, when our people and our place could no longer sustain us.

I was seeing the streets and houses and factories, and I knew we would go to the Springfield Section, because I had spent a lifetime hearing about the city. Jacksonville came up in conversations like the weather. Farmers' laconic voices always spoke of Jacksonville in the same helpless and fatalistic way. It was a fact of their lives. They had to do it. *Everybody* had to do it. Sooner or later everybody ended up in the Springfield Section, and once they were there, they loved it and hated it at the same time, loved it because it was hope, hated it because it was not home.

"It's some good, some bad, I reckon."

"A man *can* make a dollar there."

"And Godamighty, I tell you the truth being able to git up in the morning like that and turn you on some water or piss right there where you sleep, well Godamighty."

"Yeah, but I cain't get used to hearing the feller next door ever time he breaks wind."

"Or walk out the front door ever morning of your life and see right across the road that it's five or six other front doors looking dead at you."

"Still, it *is* nice to give water in the house."

They loved *things* the way only the very poor can. They would have thrown away their kerosene lamps for light bulbs in a second. They would have abandoned their wood stoves for stoves that burned anything you did not have to chop. For a refrigerator they would have broken their safes and burned them in the fireplace, which fireplace they would have sealed forever if they could have stayed warm any other way.

But it seemed dreadfully unnatural to them to stand on their front porch and be able to talk to somebody else standing on *his* front porch. It sometimes happened back in the county that a man could *see* another house from his front porch, but not often. In the city, though, they were forever cheek to jowl. They felt like animals in a pen. It was, they said, no way for a man to live. But that was not the worst part of the city. In a way that was beyond saying, what they missed the most was their county's old, familiar smell: pine sap rising in trees, the tassels of corn topping out, the hard, clean bite of frost on dead and broken cotton stalks.

Everything everywhere in the city was tainted, however faintly, with the odor of combustion. To their country noses it seemed that a little oily gas had been added to everything. They could smell it vaguely in their clothes; they could taste it in the food. It got into the drinking water and onto their hair. It hung about over the streets, a blue fog, undulating and layered.

Finally, after a little while in the city they started to long for the society of animals. They caught themselves at odd moments thinking about hogs or goats or calves.

But there was nothing to be done for all that, and everybody knew it. The little shotgun row houses were waiting in the Springfield Section and the factories were waiting and they knew their time was coming—maybe there would be many times before it was over—for them to fill the houses and offer themselves up to the factories.

In a matter of hours after we got off the Greyhound bus mama had us settled into one of the shotgun row houses. The thing was about twenty feet wide, split down the middle with a narrow hallway on either side of which were tiny, criblike rooms, four of them, one of them a kitchen with a two-burner oil stove and a midget refrigerator into which the iceman would deposit a tencent cake of ice twice a week, and one a clothes-closet-sized bathroom jammed full of a foreshortened tub and a toilet that leaned dangerously to one side and a deep tin sink that had two faucets. I was immediately curious about the faucets.

"How come it's got two?" I wanted to know.

"It's some places in the world you can git hot water out of one and cold water out of the othern."

"*All* the time?" Of all the marvels I'd seen or heard, that seemed the finest.

"All the time," she said.

We stood out in the hall for a long time looking at the faucets before I finally said, "I don't reckon them right there's got hot and cold."

"I don't reckon," she said. "We ain't quite that grand yet."

But we were grand enough. It was a dizzying thought that the toilet was right in the house. Every morning on the farm underneath every bed there was a chamber pot. My brother and I took turns carrying them out. Here you just squatted in a little closet, cranked a handle, and then everything was gone in a rush of water.

The toilet was better than the telephone, but not as mysterious. The one in the Greyhound Station was the first telephone I'd ever seen. I'd heard about them, but I never believed what I heard. I didn't believe it while mama called one of our relatives (one good thing about going from Bacon County to the Springfield Section of Jacksonville, some of your relatives would always be there, not always the same ones, but somebody would be waiting. On any day of my life, including the day I was born, I've had blood kin in Jacksonville. I do today) and the relative mama spoke to gave her another number to call and we took a long ride on a stinking city bus out Main Street to

Eighth and east on Eighth to Phoenix Avenue, where on a narrow dark street the landlord's overseer (he could only be called an overseer, never a manager) met us on the porch of one of the shotgun houses. He got mama's money, holding matches while she carefully counted it out of her cloth purse.

Everything was new and grand, even the things that did not work, and that made up a little for daddy not being with us. Mama said that daddy was supposed to finish up the crop year and that Uncle Alton would manage to look after her things. Uncle Alton remains the most beautifully stoic and courageous man I've ever known. He inevitably found the time and the wherewithal to do whatever was asked of him. Years later, when mama got bone cancer and had to stay in bed a year in a full body cast, Uncle Alton took me in with his houseful of children, keeping me and loving me as one of his own.

Shortly after we were in the house, mama gave us one of her terse, elliptical explanations of how things were.

"Me and your daddy's separated," she said.

"Separated?" I said.

"Yes," she said.

"Separated from what?" I said.

"Each other," she said.

Well, hell, I knew they were separated from each other. Hadn't I just been on a bus for three hours? It would be awhile before I understood she was talking about more than distance.

In a little over a week daddy showed up in the middle of the night. My brother and I were sleeping in the same bed when we heard the banging at the front door. We knew immediately that it was daddy. He was doing some serious begging out there on the front porch. But mama's voice was coming low and hard and abrupt right behind his as he wildly tried to explain why he had shot the mantelshelf off the fireplace.

As soon as I knew he was sober and heard him *asking* to come through the door instead of kicking the door off its hinges, I went back to sleep. During the night I woke up several times and drowsily followed the course of the argument. Once he was squatted out in the moonlight, his hat pushed back on his head, singing an old Jimmie Rodgers song. He had one of those good country voices: part drunk, part hound dog, part angel. The next time I woke up he was whispering ninety miles a minute on the other side of the front door; on this side mama was whispering the same way. Just as I was falling asleep again, one of them giggled. Sometime just before day I woke up and found the little house shaking, the thin walls humming with a low, lilting croon, a lovely sound that put me happily and profoundly back to sleep.

We all ate breakfast the next morning jammed together in the kitchen. Daddy was silent and contrite. Mama was sullen and full of frowns, darkly muttering so that only a word or two came through to us now and then. Fascinated, we all listened to grumble grumble *shotgun* grumble grumble grumble *kill* grumble *never* grumble grumble *split his* grumble. Daddy's face went tighter and his mouth thinner, but he didn't say anything.

But he might as well have gone on and said whatever was on his mind, though, because mama ran him off again anyway before the day was half over. He went quickly and seemed to take pleasure in his going, the hot urgency of the night before considerably cooled. I don't know how long he might have got to hang around if she had not caught him bubbling a bottle of whiskey in front of the green wavy mirror in the bathroom. He dearly loved to drink in front of a mirror. I don't know why. He never said; I never asked. But mama had caught him more than once at the mirror. He was pretty helpless and easy to trap there, his head thrown back, his eyes walled and turned down, trying to see the bottle raised over his face. His vision would be blurred from watering eyes, his other senses warped and crippled from whiskey roaring in his blood. Which was a hell of a time to have somebody run right up his back. Which is exactly what mama would do. He could come home drunk and not catch much heat at all, but if mama caught him bubbling a bottle in front of the mirror, she went right up his back.

The sight of whiskey in her house drove her to inspired heights of outrage and violence, so much so that she would sometimes take daddy right off his feet with a broom handle or whatever she could lay hand to. He barely missed taking a plate in the ear as he went out the door this time, his bottle in one hand, his hat in the other. The tension and anger coming off the two of them like sparks off a stove brought the unmistakable smell of grapefruit into the house. It was the first time, but it was not to be the last.

Mama went straight to King Edward Cigar Factory for a job and got it. The women of the Springfield Section, at least the Bacon County women, all worked for King Edward. Women were thought to be defter and quicker at handling the various processes—filler, rolling leaf, packaging—and since the factory was right there in the same section of town where the Georgia women lived, they ended up working for King Edward almost exclusively.

Mama's job was to spread a single leaf of tobacco evenly on a metal plate of a machine which in turn rolled previously shaped filler into a finished cigar. She did piecework: the more cigars she rolled, the more money she made. I cannot remember how much she was paid, but it was little enough so that when help was offered to keep us fed, we were glad to accept it.

What little help there was came in the form of food baskets and secondhand clothing from various charitable agencies, including the Baptist Church. Sometimes it came on holidays, sometimes not. But whenever it came and whatever it was, it always looked good and felt even better.

That may seem strange to those who have a singularly distorted understanding of the rural Southerner's attitude toward charity. The people in the South I come from, those who knew what it meant to be forever on the edge of starvation, took whatever they could get and made whatever accommodations they had to make in their heads and hearts to do it.

Back in the county there was no charity. People gave things to each other, peas because they couldn't sell them or use them, same with tomatoes, sweet corn, milk, and sometimes even a piece of meat because it was going to turn rank in the smokehouse before they could eat it. But nothing was made out of giving or receiving. It was never called charity or even a gift. It was just the natural order of things for people whose essential problem, first and last, was survival.

They accepted what was offered them in Jacksonville the same way, as the natural order of things. We ate the food with relish and wore the clothes with pride. Farmers relocated from Georgia, most of whom had spent their lives working somebody else's land, felt right at home with overalls that were perfectly good except for maybe a rip in one knee and a section in the bib made rotten by bleach.

While mama went off to the cigar factory every morning at six and my brother went off to school at eight, I went out into the street with the other children too young for school. I was bigger than most of them because not only would I soon be six, I was also big for my age. Most of the shotgun houses were empty during the day. Everybody who was old enough to quit school was at work, women and men alike; the rest were in school, except for those of us too young for work or school and so spent the day trying to find odd jobs or stealing or pressing flesh in unthinkably erotic games of our own devising inside the empty shotgun houses.

My best friend was Junior Lister, who was not a junior in the sense that his name was the same as his father's. Junior, a particularly common name in Bacon County, was his real and only name.

"Shit no," he told me. "It don't stand for nothing. It ain't nothing else there. I ain't even got a damn initial."

Junior had a head as blunt as a snake's, with a broad, flat forehead, that he claimed he could break a brick with. I saw him butt through several things, including a door. And while I never saw him break a brick, I never doubted he could. His neck was as broad as his head so that the whole thing from his ears down drove right into his meaty little shoulders. He was bigger than I was, but then he was bigger than any of the other children who roamed the broken streets of the Springfield Section during the day. Junior had become six in January and hadn't been old enough to start school the previous year. So besides being a naturally big boy, who was already showing the arms and shoulders that would make him the terror of

Bacon County a decade later, he was also older than any of the
rest of us. He was meaner, too. He smoked cigarettes and
cursed and ran down little girls, groping them right in the
street, and was afraid of nobody, not even his parents, who pe-
riodically beat him savagely whether he had done anything or
not, because as all our parents said, a beating will loosen a
child's hide and let him grow.

It was a great thing in the neighborhood to become Junior's
friend and wonderful beyond anything to be his best buddy,
which I became shortly after I met him. I've never known precisely why it happened, but I suspect it was because it never occurred to me to question anything he said or did. He was
seldom without a scheme, and I was always anxious to do
what I could to help.

"Can you git out tonight for a little while?"

We were sitting on a curbstone on Phoenix Avenue. It was
sundown, already an hour past the time when I should have
been home.

"I reckon," I said.

"I got a place I can sell a set of hubcaps off a new Plymouth
car," he said. "It's got to be a set, though. Two or three won't
do us a bit of good."

He never stole anything unless he knew where he could sell it.
And if he saw something particularly nice that he knew he could
steal fairly easily, he would go out and find somebody willing to
pay. I found out later that was what happened with the hubcaps. He had seen some that were eminently stealable, and by
asking around he heard that his older brother had a friend who
was building a car that new Plymouth hubcaps would fit.

"What time?" I said.

"How bout nine?"

"Ma ain't gone let me out of the house at nine," I said. "We
either got to do it by seven-thirty or else wait till leven."

Mama would be deep in an exhausted sleep by eleven and I
could sneak out. There was no need to explain anything to Junior. We'd been through it all before. My brother, who slept in
the same bed with me, wouldn't say anything about it, either.
He didn't care what I did as long as I didn't want to do it with

him. Boys from the farm didn't have anything to do much with their younger brothers, especially when there was as much as four years' difference in their ages, unless the older one was feeling especially violent and didn't have anybody else handy to beat.

"I'll meet you here at leven," Junior said. "It's over yonder by Eighth Street. We oughta be back in a hour."

It was easy enough to get out of the house, as I knew it would be. Mama was lying on the bed, one arm thrown across her eyes, when I came in.

"Where you been?" she said, without taking her arm down.

"We was playing marvels," I said. Two or three years later I would be shocked to find out that other people in the world pronounced the word *marbles*. "I didn't see how late it was gittin'."

"You ain't got no marvels," she said.

That was true. I'd given up my marbles when I started to steal. The two didn't seem to go together.

"No, ma'am," I said. It wouldn't do to lie about anything she had direct knowledge of. Mama would get up and beat you no matter how tired she was for telling an obvious lie. "Junior let me borry some of hisn."

"You ain't been playing with Junior Lister again," she said.

"No, ma'am," I said. "He was just passing by where I was at."

"You ain't gone make it in life as a liar. You a sorry liar."

"Yes, ma'am," I said.

She didn't move on the bed, not even her arm covering her eyes, while she told me the stock was bad. Stock was the final leaf the cigar was rolled in. Mama's job was to spread that leaf out smoothly, nothing else, just that single spreading movement, about 6,000 times a day. If the leaves were soft and pliable, she came home carrying nothing more serious than exhaustion in her bones. But if the leaves were brittle and broken, if they resisted being spread on the metal plate, then you kept your mouth shut and walked softly around her. No strategy was too complicated if it kept you from being noticed. On days when stock was bad, you could easily end up paying the price for 6,000 broken leaves of tobacco, for 6,000 moments of frustration that had the effect of producing in her a crushing anxiety and paranoia.

Which is pretty much the same effect it had on the other women in the neighborhood. That was why I knew the stock had been bad that day before I got home. That's why I stayed out on the street as long as I thought I possibly could without getting my head caught between her knees. I'd seen kids being beaten and slapped about all afternoon in the Springfield Section by women you could smell as far away as you could see them. They smelled, stunk, of tobacco, their hair, their clothes, their skins, probably even their hearts.

"You gotta git another clock," Junior said when I met him at midnight.

"She had a headache," I said. "She couldn't go to sleep."

"That bad stock," he said. It was not a question but simple affirmation. He had caught a couple of licks from his own mama.

"Where is it at we're going?" I said when he headed off toward Eighth.

"Market," he said.

"That's a long ways," I said.

"All the time'll be walking over there and gittin back. The job ain't gone take but a minute."

When we'd got to Eighth, we went west to Market Street and then turned left. It was in the third block, a little confectionery store, not as long nor as wide as our house. A brand-new Plymouth was at the curb in front of the store.

"Old lady that runs the place lives in the back."

"You mean she lives right here."

"We ain't got nothing to worry about."

I was glad to hear it, but not entirely convinced, because the store was so short and the curb so close to the front door, I was sure she would hear us, and I told Junior so.

He didn't even look up at me as he squatted beside the right front wheel with a screwdriver. "You ain't been caught yet, have you?" he asked.

"What do you want me to do?" I said.

"Just cetch it when it pops off."

I did. We moved to the next one. He worked the screwdriver and another hubcap slid off into my hands. He'd had some practice at it, and he was good. Too good, because when he popped the third one, I hadn't yet got into position and it hit the pavement and rolled. Simultaneously with the hubcap hitting the pavement, a light came on in the rear of the store.

In a flat, inflectionless voice while he moved to the last hubcap, Junior cursed people who couldn't hold onto things.

"I give you the easiest goddamn part of it," he said.

But I was babbling by then. "A light's come on. They turned on a light. It's. . . ."

"You ain't got nothing to worry about. Shut up and squat down here."

Whether the light made him nervous and fumble-fisted, or whether it was stuck, Junior couldn't pop it right off. He was mumbling and prying at the hubcap when the front door of the store opened and an old, cracked, woman's voice floated out to us on the night air.

"Boys, please don't steal my hubcaps. Please don't. Ohhh, boys."

The old lady had turned on the lights in the front of the store, and we were very near where she sat now in her wheelchair sharply silhouetted in the door.

"Junior," I said. "She's in a wheelchair."

Junior looked up, his face radiant in the dim light from the store. "I know," he said. "She ain't even got a telephone neither." He stood up with the last hubcap, looked over casually at the old lady, who begged in a continuous broken voice. He kicked the tire a couple of times. "Too bad we cain't steal the whole car." He ambled off down the sidewalk, and I followed him.

Half a block away, I turned and called: "I'm sorry, lady."

Junior stopped and stared at me. "If you so sorry, it may be we oughta take'm back. Course Bernie's gone give us eight dollars cash money for'm."

"It didn't hurt to tell that poor old thing I was sorry," I said and kept on walking.

There were a few weeks in which we sold to the same man we stole from. The man owned a junkyard, three square blocks of parts of tractors and parts of cars and parts of washing machines, seemingly a little bit of everything in the world that was made of metal. He bought his own copper from us with great enthusiasm. He would buy any kind of metal, but he paid the most for copper. He was nuts about any kind of copper.

"I found out where they is some copper," Junior said to me one day at our place on the curbstone.

He had found out about the copper being piled up under a shed, which not only had no doors, it had no walls.

"We can just walk in there and git us some and then sell it back to'm. They like that pipe the best. If we can steal us a mess of them copper pipes, we'll be in high cotton."

And we did. We stole and we sold. The man we sold it to knew that it was stolen. How else could children our age, a couple of six-year-olds, get so much copper? But he didn't know where it was coming from and thought he didn't want to know. He didn't even want to know our names. He just beamed when we came in with his copper. He'd pay us—knocking down the price he would have had to pay anybody but children, which we knew—and happily send us on our way.

He was glad to be getting a cheap supply of copper, and we were glad to oblige his larceny. But it couldn't go on forever. Either Junior or I or maybe both of us had talked it around that we were stealing at the back door and selling at the front door. Somebody called the cops—probably a kid Junior had dragged down the street by his heels, he being habitually disposed to beat up on any child he could run down without too much trouble.

The cops came to his house but found nothing. They did, however, scare him witless. Both his mama and his daddy beat him, but he told me he was still so scared by the cops he hardly felt it and he had to concentrate to cry. His parents, like all the parents from Bacon County, used crying to determine when they should stop. It wasn't how loud the crying was, but a whole complexity of factors: how genuinely contrite did it sound, how hopeless, how agonized and full of grief, how well did the child understand that he was worthless and that only by the Grace of God and the slash of the whip, both administered for reasons of love, could he expect to get near people again, most of whom—he was given to understand—were his moral superior. That Junior was able to bring his voice to the proper sound after he'd just been visited by cops of a foreign country astounded me.

"If I don't cry when daddy whips me," Junior said, "if I don't git it right, he never will let up. There for a while when I couldn't git my mind on it, he had me down on the floor whoppin me hard as he could with that razor strop. He's beatin me across the head and everything, hard as he can swing, and all the time he's yelling: 'Don't play with me, Junior. Don't play with me.'"

It made a believer out of Junior. He said we ought to bear down and get us something regular to work at. Many of the children had jobs, an hour or two a day cleaning something up in a store or cleaning up the pen where the stores put their garbage, anything a kid could be trusted with doing, and doing quickly, since it was against the law to work them too long.

A few days later I was out in the end of Phoenix Avenue and I passed a little grocery store that had a butcher shop in the back. I went inside and convinced the man who owned it that he needed me to clean up the butcher shop. The day after I went to work for him I was in the back scrubbing down the butcher's block and sweeping up the sawdust on the floor, because it was only about twenty minutes until quitting time, when a man came into the store and sprinted down between the aisles to where I was working. Everybody in the store stopped to watch, such was the look in the man's face of raw, wild desperation. When he got to the back, he came right behind the counter and slid to a stop. He was wearing faded overalls, brogans, and a felt hat. His upper lip was weighted with a heavy, stained mustache. His wrists and hands seemed much too large for his emaciated body.

"Knife," he said to me.

"Knife," I said.

"Where?" he said.

"Butcher block," I said.

I was as motionless as a stuffed bird. Only my eyes moved, and they only moved to follow him. The customers from the store, including Mr. Joseph, who owned it, came rushing back to the meat counter. They were terrified as I was, and all we could do was watch as the man went to the butcher block and withdrew from a rack nailed into the side of it a very long knife, honed until the blade was thin and sharp as a razor. He brought the knife up and jammed it into his chest. Strangely it did not go in very deep. Everybody gasped and one lady fainted when he made that first plunge. He walked in a little circle like a dog looking for a place to lie down. He walked that way for a long time, making a little track in the sawdust. The lady who fainted came around and was led away. Then the man stopped in his circle. He held the knife steady with one hand and struck it with the other hand, palm down, driving the blade a little deeper.

"He's gone puncture his heart!" one of the ladies screamed. As if on signal they all ran out of the store. Mr. Joseph, who owned the place, called back over his shoulder that he was going for the police.

The man had started circling again, but he stopped. "How come that feller to go for the police?" He no longer looked angry or desperate, only very sad. The knife had calmed him down. I remember thinking it was like medicine. He'd run in here hurting, but he slipped that blade into his chest and the pain went away. "How come him to go?" His voice was little more than a whisper; his eyes wet and bright but calm.

"I don't think you allowed to do it," I said.

"What?" he said.

"Stick youself."

When he spoke, his voice was subdued. "I reckon I shouldn't a come in here and taken his knife. That's near bout stealing."

He casually raised his open hand and tapped the knife a little deeper. After he put another little bit of the blade in his chest, he almost smiled.

"The knife ain't how come him to go for the police," I said. "You cain't stick your own self in a store or out in the middle of the field or anywhere. It's agin the law."

"Law ain't studying me," he said, beginning to circle again.

"You from Bacon County?" I asked. It was the only thing I could think of to say.

He smiled at me as he turned in his circle. "Sho now, boy." He tapped the knife a little more. He was really bleeding now, his overalls full of blood all the way to his knees.

"I'm from Bacon County, too," I said, desperate to stop him.

"I'm a Pitfield," he said.

"I'm a Crews," I said.

"I mought know your people. I probly do."

"Myrtice is my mama and Pascal is my daddy," I said, watching the door, hoping for Mr. Joseph and the police.

"I don't know," he said. "I don't know. It is some Crewses up around the Harrikin I known."

"You don't need to do this," I said. "You can always just quit an go on home." I was a little beside myself to think of something to get him to stop.

"Home," he said in a quiet, bemused voice, addressing whatever came before his eyes as he turned the circle. "It ain't nair nail left in the world where my hat is welcome."

He turned his eyes toward me. "Come over here, boy." I stood where I was. "Come on over here." I stepped closer. He leaned just perceptibly. "You don't have to worry about this. I don't want you to worry about this." I didn't say anything. "You know why it ain't no reason for you nor nobody else to worry about this?"

"Why?" I said.

"The knife feels good."

"Godamighty," I said.

"It feels good."

He said something else, but I didn't hear him. I knew it was hopeless. I could not have said it then, but I knew in my bones that he was caught in a life where the only thing left to do was what he was doing. He had told himself a story he believed, or somebody else had told it to him, a story in which the next thing that happened—the only thing that *could* happen—was the knife. It was the next thing, the right thing, the only thing, and the knife felt good. If my life to that moment had taught me nothing else, it had made me understand exactly what he meant. Talking wasn't going to do any good.

He took another little slap at the top of the knife and seemed to relax all along his bones as the blade went deep. His face grew calmer still.

"Well, I'm through with it all now," he said. He hit the knife particularly hard, and he stopped in his circle as though he had run into a stone wall. "I'm through with it. Somebody else is gone have to look after it."

Like a folding chair closing, he sank slowly to his knees. He turned his face, the whitest face I'll ever see, toward me. "I've kilt myself," he said in a flat, matter-of-fact voice.

He stayed just that way, on his knees, his bloodless face turned to me, as Mr. Joseph came running through the store with a policeman. As they came around the counter, the man gave himself a little more of the blade and pitched forward on his face into a ring of blood-soaked sawdust.

The cop, red-faced and breathing heavily, walked over and turned his face out of the sawdust, glanced at it briefly, and stood up.

I went over to Mr. Joseph and gave him my apron. "Quittin," I said, and rushed out of the store.

Shortly after I quit my job in the butcher shop, we were evicted. Mama came home one evening and there was a notice nailed to the door explaining it. She glanced at it a moment and threw it in the garbage. The overseer came by four or five days later to inquire about our plans. But the stock had been bad that day and he never should have come.

"I seen it," mama said.

"You ain't got but four more days," he said.

"Four more days to what?"

"Move out."

"I ain't moving out," she said.

"We'll just have to start tearing the roof off then because the landlord's building something else here. He'll come down and talk to you hisself."

"Anytime he wants to," she said, and went back to the bed to lie down but not without first telling the overseer that he was the sorriest man ever to shit behind two shoes.

The landlord, a short, plump man with tiny feet and tiny hands, showed up two days later.

"It's just me and these younguns here, and we ain't got nowhere else to go," mama said.

"I'm very grieved to hear that," he said, "but I'm afraid we'll have to tear the roof off anyway."

He stayed around for another half hour and told mama he was very grieved about her life and what was happening in it. Finally, he waved as he was leaving and said over his shoulder in a pleasant singsong voice: "We won't put you in the sidewalk, Mizz Crews, if you don't make us. No sireeee."

Even though mama had never missed a rent payment, or even been late with one, when I came home later that same week from selling newspapers, a job I had got at the *Jacksonville Journal*, everything we owned, which was precious little because all the splintered, stick furniture belonged to the landlord, was piled out on the sidewalk. The doors and windows were nailed shut. It was just beginning to mist, but by the time mama got home from work it was raining hard. She was soaking wet after walking from where the bus let her off. Everything we owned was soaked. It was cold. My brother and I were sitting on the front steps of the boarded-up house. Mama had stopped by the store on the way home. The bag of groceries she was holding had split. A package of Spam was showing out of the bottom.

"Junior's mama said we could stay over with them," I said.

"I'm staying right here," she said, walking past my brother and me. She set the sack down on the floor and without any apparent difficulty ripped off the boards that had been nailed over the front door. "You two boys bring that stuff back in here."

My brother and I both were scared to death that the land-lord or his man would show up that night. If they did, neither of us had any doubt that mama would attack. In her state after seeing her things pitched onto the sidewalk, she would have chewed their throats out. Fortunately, they did not come that night. But they did come the next day, and when we got home, all our stuff was on the sidewalk again. Mama sent word to Junior's mama that we would stay there until we found a place, if it was all right. In two days we had another house, identical to the one we had been forced out of.

The landlord never did get around to tearing down the house we'd been living in before, nor had we expected him to. Within the week another family was living there. If a landlord in the Springfield Section got an offer of $2 more than he had been getting, he'd throw one family out and let another family in. It was done all the time. With such regularity, in fact, that a pile of things—sheets and pillows and pans and maybe a chest of drawers and clothes—piled on the sidewalk turned nobody's head. Unless you happened to know and like the people who had been evicted. Then you tried to help. Usually, if it was not in your block, you ignored it.

Shortly after we had been evicted, daddy—not knowing we had moved—crawled in through one of the windows of the little house and ended up scrambling around in the bed with the man and woman who had moved in behind us, whom it nearly scared to death. It scared daddy pretty good, too.

"Scared my pony," he said. "Damn if I didn't think he meant to kill me."

He had come banging on our door at ten o'clock Saturday morning. Mama let him in because the stock had been good the past few days and also because it had been over two weeks since she had let him in the last time.

Daddy had been around pretty regularly of late. He had even *stayed* with us a few times. But generally it was swooning and crooning on the sidewalk and at the bedroom window, or whispering frantically through doors and walls. And then, once he was inside, it was a continual mad rush through the house, senseless and crazed.

But I never thought too much about it all, one way or the other. Certainly it did not cause me any shame. How could it when half the fathers and husbands at any given moment were swooning and crooning along the sidewalks and at the bedroom windows of the Springfield Section and later rushing madly about, senseless and crazed? Junior's own daddy, Leland Lister, almost never used any other entrance to his house except the side window after first giving himself a medium to heavy hurt with whiskey. He would immediately attack his family savagely until he had punched them all enough to make them listen. Then he would commence to say in a broken and poorly voice that he was doing the best he could, saying that it wasn't his fault. He always ended with: "I'm just like Godamighty made me." All the men of Springfield Section went about it pretty much the same way. Daddy was neither better nor worse than the rest. He was simply one of them.

But finally the night came when not only was the fight different from any I had heard before, it was the worst. It lasted longer, too, about five hours. It would stop for a little while and then start again. The other fights had risen straight to the top and exploded. This one rose and fell, rose and fell. When the screaming quit, a murderous murmuring started up.

Sometime toward the end of that exhausted night, daddy came into the room where I was alone on the bed. My brother had gone to the bathroom and stayed, because you could never be sure the fight would not spill over into whatever room you happened to try to hide out in. Except the bathroom. For some reason the fighting never came into the bathroom after you.

Strangely, daddy was almost sober. His eyes were red as coals. He seemed to stand with a curious resignation, curious because when he had been drinking, he stood and walked like a bandit, a kind of strut that invited violence.

"Well," he said, "I reckon that about does it."

He did not sit down and left my door open, through which a wedge of dim light fell from the hall. He stood next to my bed but did not look at me.

"You all right?" I asked.

When he had been drinking, he sometimes thought there

were men waiting outside to kill him. When he was like that, mama would always ask him if he was all right. The question popped out of my mouth because it scared me to have him come into my room like that in the middle of a fight. He'd never done it before.

"It ain't nothing the matter with me," he said.

But I'd heard him say the same thing when he was shaking with fear of the men outside armed with shotguns, men who were not outside at all.

"I ain't gone be by to see you no more," he said.

"Never?" I said.

"Never," he said.

I thought about that for a moment. It was clearly impossible. "Daddy," I said, "you *got* to come by."

"Cain't," he said. "Have the law on me I do. You ma's gittin a divorce. She got a peace bond on me now."

It didn't make sense to me. I knew what a divorce was well enough, but when he mixed it with a peace bond, the purpose of which I had no notion, and said too that he would never see me again, it only scared and confused me.

"I never was your daddy, but I tried to be one to you." He shook his head. "It just wasn't in me, though."

I felt myself burn all along my nerves. Was not my daddy? *Not* my daddy? Is that what I heard?

"What?"

I have lost most of the rest of whatever passed between us, lost it in the same way that I lost the fact that he was my stepfather. I must have known it, must have heard it somewhere, perhaps more than once, but if I did, I somehow managed to forget it.

But I remember clearly how it all ended.

"My daddy was who?"

"My brother."

"Brother?" I could only think of my own brother. It didn't make sense.

"I was your uncle."

"Uncle?" I could only think of Uncle Alton. It didn't make sense.

"I won't be by to see you no more," he said. "I won't be seeing you." I didn't for a second believe him because it made no sense.

But he was as good as his word, and it taught me not to give a damn for what makes sense. I didn't see him again until I was out of the Marine Corps and going to the University of Florida. I had not thought of him in years when I woke up one Saturday morning determined to do whatever was necessary to see him.

I found him in the Springfield Section of Jacksonville not far from where I lost him. He was sitting in the back of a tiny store, huddled beside a stove in a huge overcoat. He was very nervous. He did not want to talk. I left minutes after I got there. We never touched each other, not even to shake hands.

CHAPTER 11

In the middle of summer, five months after we moved to Jacksonville, mama announced that we were moving back to the farm. She had managed to put a down payment on a little place about a quarter of a mile from where we used to live. It was not at all like the Williams place. The house was unpainted; the mule stable and corncrib were badly slanted. There was no tobacco barn because the place had no tobacco allotment. Many nights I got myself to sleep by seeing how many stars I could count through the shingles of the roof, and when things were slow during the day, I would fish for chickens. But I had to be careful that mama didn't find me with a fishhook tied to a piece of tobacco string and baited with a kernel of corn hanging through a crack in the floor down to where the chickens scratched under the house.

The farm was a little less than thirty acres in cultivation, and so we only had one mule, whose teeth showed him to be probably over twenty, which meant he was on the downhill side of his life. A mule man can always tell within a year or two how old a mule is. And if a mule is young enough, he can tell his age within a few months.

A mule has a full set of teeth when he's born. But when he is two years old, he sheds two of the teeth right in the front. A good mule man can tell if he's shed those two front teeth, in which case he is between two and three years old. A really good man can tell if those teeth have just grown back in or if they've been back in the mule's mouth for several months. The next year, when he's three, the mule sheds two more teeth, one on each side of the two he shed the year before. From then on the mule sheds two teeth a year until he's five years old. That's the last time he sheds.

Then you have to go to the cups to tell his age. Mules and horses have little trenches, called cups, in the top of each tooth. Eating corn and picking up sand when they graze on grass wear down those cups. Each year they become shallower, and by the time he's ten he becomes what farmers call smooth-mouthed. When the cups are entirely gone, the mule starts to get a noticeable overbite—buck-toothed. From the age of ten until the animal dies, it becomes progressively harder to get his age with much certainty. Unless you happen to be a real mule man. If you are, you can check the angle of inclination of the teeth and get his age within a year or two. About the time the mule is thirteen or fourteen, he has become about as buck-toothed as he's going to get. Then instead of looking in the mule's mouth, you get behind him, squat down so you have a low-angle vision of his legs and haunches, and have somebody lead him away from you so you can see how he tracks. The mule man wants to see how he walks. Does he favor a leg? Do his hindquarters "drag," that is, seem to be pulled along rather than offer the driving power they should have? Does anything on the animal seem to be sore, particularly his back?

After the first ten years, the rest of it depends upon the mule man's eye and his experience. Usually the mule traders who judge the age of very old mules are themselves very old men. They sometimes make bad mistakes, because some old mules will look very young, having a high sheen on their coats, smooth, tight-muscled bodies, and a spirit in their hearts that kept their heads high, kept them fast walkers and mean. An old mule usually will not kick you and he will not bite you. But there are exceptions, and it was on these exceptions that the best of traders sometimes got cheated.

But that wasn't the only way to get cheated. There were men— a few—who specialized in reconditioning a mule's mouth. And as is always the case, there was one man who was better at it than anybody else in the county. All the other men charged about $1 a head to work on a mule's mouth. But the man who was the recognized expert at it charged $5, and he was worth it. Nobody looked down upon these men for what they did. They had a special and perfected craft, and they exercised it for anybody willing to pay the freight.

What the mouth doctors did was to put the cups back into the teeth with an electric drill that had a bit about the size of a match stick. They just put a twist on the upper lip of the mule so he would stand still and then drilled a little trench in the top of each tooth. When that was done, they stained the trench so that it looked as it would if it were the original. All the mouth doctors had a special stain, and they would die and go to hell before divulging how it was made. It was common knowledge that the base of these stains came from green walnuts, but whatever the ultimate ingredients, the best stains could not be taken, not even with sandpaper. An old mule that's been recapped is allowed to stand in the lot for a week or two before he's taken to market. Any mule, no matter how old he is, that is not worked for a couple of weeks gets as frisky as a colt, his ears are always up, and he farts a lot. It is an act of faith in Bacon County that "a farting mule is a good mule." Such a mule will kick you, too. If it's all done right, it takes a good man not to get beaten in a trade for a mule whose mouth has been worked on by somebody who knows what he's doing.

We had no such trouble with the mule we bought when we got back to Bacon County. Every physical attitude, every aspect of the way he moved showed he had done his time between the trace chains and then some. He'd even gone gray in the head. As young as I was, I was glad Pete—that was his name—didn't know he'd been sold to us for $20.

Pete, with that old gray head and a mouth full of ground-down and bucked teeth, had also been cupped, which shamed Mr. Willis as much as if somebody had spit in his face. Mr. Willis was the hired man mama had got to come and live with us to tend the farm. He must have been fifty, but with his body still ropy with muscle, carrying almost no fat, so reticent that he rarely spoke unless spoken to, and never in a hurry. The house could have been burning down and he would have moved as slow as grass growing. Mama would sometimes say something to him about working a little faster, and he would stop completely, turn to her, and say in his grave, considered voice: "Mizz Crews, I ain't made of iron nor steel nor run by lectricity," then he would methodically resume whatever he was doing in his same slow way.

He'd been a hired hand all his life, but he was formal to the point of being courtly. I don't even remember his first name; everybody called him Mr. Willis. He was a man whose schedule was as regular as the ticking of a clock. The first thing he did in the morning was take his hat off the bedpost and put it on his head; the last thing he did at night was to take it off and put it back on the post. If you wanted to see him without his hat, you had to catch him asleep. Which nobody ever did because he got up with the chickens.

He slept with a tiny piece of tobacco in his mouth, about the size of a pencil eraser. After he got his hat on, he took out the chew he'd slept with, which he said with utter conviction kept a man's stomach free from worms, and replaced it with a half a plug of Day's Work, keeping it in his mouth all day except for meals. Sometimes, apparently forgetting to take it out, he would eat with the tobacco bulging like a tumor in his right jaw.

He was also—I think—the cleanest man I ever knew. I say I *think* he was the cleanest man I ever knew because like everything else he did, he made his toilet in absolute privacy. After his hat was on his head, he filled a syrup bucket full of water from the well, went off through the field to a little head of woods about a quarter of a mile away, carrying with him rags torn from worn-out bed sheets stuffed in his pockets. He would stay down there for an hour and come back carrying an empty bucket and no rags. My brother and I went back to where he washed and there were white rags hanging everywhere, from limbs of trees, from bushes, carefully spread out to dry. Several cakes of homemade lye soap would be wedged in the crooks of trees and wrapped in the rags be washed in. Eventually a quarter acre of woods was decorated with white, various-shaped rags. And yet every morning he would carry another pocket of rags with him. When he came to breakfast, his skin was red and scrubbed to glowing. In the year he farmed with us, I never remember him saying anything at breakfast. It was not in his schedule. He ate slowly, chewing slowly and with the precision of a metronome. He never drank anything while he was eating, but the moment his jaws stopped he lifted the quart of iced tea he insisted upon for every meal and drank it down slowly, without stopping. We always stopped to watch him do it, his throat pumping impossibly until it was all gone. Then he would abruptly set the jar down and leave the table to go to the lot to put the gear on Pete.

Later we would see him and Pete in the field. Mama, looking at him through the window, would say: "Damn, if you wouldn't have to set a peg out there to see if he's moving."

Pete would stop about every seventy yards, and Mr. Willis would stop with him, standing quietly between the handles of the plow until Pete would start up again in about five minutes. We had bought Pete from an eighty-year-old farmer, and Pete had learned to stop about every seventy yards so the old man could rest two or three minutes before going on. Pete had been doing it for twenty years or more, and Mr. Willis saw no reason to change Pete's ways.

Mama, short on patience as usual, suggested that Mr. Willis take a strap to Pete when he stopped for the rest periods. Mr. Willis thought about it for a minute and finally said: "Mizz Crews, Pete's as old as I am, turned as many rows as I have, and I ain't got it in me to beat this old man." Mr. Willis clucked and Pete leaned into his collar and the two of them moved off down the row at the same ambling gait for another seventy yards.

But all mules, young and old, had their ways. You got to know them like people, what they liked and what they didn't, what they would put up with and what they wouldn't. And you remembered them like people, just as vividly.

The most intense love affair I've ever known was between two mules we owned the year I finally left the farm for good. Doc, a big iron-gray horse mule, and Otha, a little red mare mule about 300 pounds lighter than Doc, were matched mules. They had been broken together, trained to move in their harness with precision and smoothness.

Matched mules are nearly always the same weight because if they are not and they are asked to pull something really heavy, the bigger mule lunges into his harness, bellying down behind his collar, and simply snatches the smaller mule back against the doubletree, an iron bar to which their trace chains are ultimately fastened, and, in effect, this loses all the pulling power of the lighter mule. It becomes a seesaw, with one mule lunging and then the other. The bigger mule isn't pulling *with* but *against* the one he's in double harness with.

Not so with Doc and Otha. Doc waited. He compensated. The two of them would, slow as breathing, tighten their traces together, leaning into their collars. When I've seen Doc turn— even in the middle of the worst kind of pull—and look at his fine little mare mule beside him giving all she had to give, I knew he was *thinking* how best to help her, how best to take whatever part of the load he could take off her. I always knew he thought about her a lot. *Thought.* A deliberate word. I can't prove it's true, but then most of what I believe I can't prove.

We always had to take both Doc and Otha to the field even if we planned to work only one of them. We had to hitch the one not being worked so that they would never be out of sight of one another. If we took one out of the lot without the other, or for any reason made it so they could not see each other, they would literally rip themselves apart in an effort to get back together: knock down fences, go through barbed wire, cut their heads and chests slamming through stables.

I've never doubted the love between Doc and Otha. As everybody knows, mules are hybrids and cannot breed. Who, but a fool, though, would maintain that breeding is an indispensable part of love? Doc and Otha were the same age, both five-year-olds. One of them had to die first. I've always been grateful I was not there to see the one that was left.

I was unfortunate enough to see Pete almost die. We'd cut a lot of green grass and put it in the corncrib to dry. Somehow the door to the crib was left open, and Pete got in there with all that corn and green grass and just about ate himself to death as old mules will sometimes do. Mr. Willis came to the

house and told mama she had better come out to the crib and
see Pete.

"What ails'm?" she asked.

"Swol up," he said.

"Swol up?"

"That old man's foundered?"

"Mr. Willis, for God's sake, spit it out. What is it you trying
to say?"

What he was trying to say was that Pete was hideously swollen in the belly and legs and that he would very probably die,
being as old as he was.

"Them old fellers cain't take it much. He was younger, he'd
have a better chance."

"What are we gone do?" mama said.

"Best we can, I reckon," he said.

Mr. Willis' best was good enough as it turned out. I went
with him down to the creek, walking very slowly, leading Pete,
who waddled like a duck. Even Pete's face seemed swollen
from eating all night. And he insisted on stopping every seventy yards or so to rest awhile even though he wasn't pulling
anything.

Mr. Willis took Pete out belly deep in cool running water
and hitched him there. "We'll just let that old man stand there
in that water a few hours and see don't that help him some."

Pete stood in the water until sundown, and when Mr. Willis
took him out of the water, he didn't look much different from
the way he did when we put him in.

"Didn't go down much, did he?" said Mr. Willis.

"He don't look like he went down none," I said. Mr. Willis
had taken out his pocketknife. "What you aim to do with that
knife?" I asked.

"I'm gone bore some holes in'm and let that swelling out."

"You better ask mama before you go boring holes in the
mule," I said.

His saying he was going to bore holes to let the swelling out
scared me. I had an immediate vision of Mr. Willis up under
Pete's swollen and drum-tight belly boring away with his

knife, stabbing great gouty holes through the flesh, and black poisonous fluid pouring down over his head and shoulders as he did so. I was considerably relieved to see him bend to Pete's hooves.

"What you do is bore some holes down here where the hair meets the hoof." He grunted while he worked. "Let'm give a little blood."

"Will he be all right then?"

As was his way, he quit entirely with what he was doing, stood up, and turned to face me. "Well," he said, after he had considered the question for some time, "he might and he might not."

He put about five holes in each hoof while Pete, stunned from eating all night and standing in water all day, didn't even flinch as the blood started trickling over his hooves. Finally, he began to stamp and paw the ground.

"See, that right there smarts," said Mr. Willis, "and gits'm to stompin his feet. Now, he'll either die or he'll git better."

Pete must have bled two quarts before the wounds closed up. The next morning the swelling had gone down a lot, and in a few days Pete was back in the field working. Pete had all that land to break by himself, and it was a killer. The place had lain fallow for a year, so there were no stalks to cut and rake and burn, but there were weeds: cockleburs and coffee weeds and dog fennel. The fields had to be burned first and then disked with a plow we called a cutaway harrow. Only then could it be turned. But eventually it was done, because although both Pete and Mr. Willis were slow, they were steady.

After Pete was over his sickness from eating too much, I talked to Mr. Willis about the cure, something that had been bothering me.

"Didn't it hurt Pete to cut his feet that way?" I asked.

"I reckon so," he said.

"It was a awful thing to have to do to'm."

Mr. Willis thought about it for a little and said: "No, it weren't."

"It weren't?"

"Not awful as dying," he said. "Nothing else to do. Things

git easy when it's nothing else to do. I known that when I weren't no biggern you are, boy."

When something was necessary, it was done, whether to a mule or to a child or to your own mother did not matter. People in Bacon County never did anything worse to their stock than they were sometimes forced to do to themselves. Mr. Willis was no exception. I never knew him to be sick (despite the fact that he bathed naked in the woods out of a syrup bucket in freezing weather), but he *did* have very bad teeth, perhaps from sucking on tobacco day and night. His reticence and courtly manner never left him except when the pain from his teeth was on him bad.

He lived in a shedlike little room off the side of the house. The room didn't have much in it: a ladder-back chair, a kerosene lamp, a piece of broken glass hanging on the wall over a pan of water where he shaved as often as once a week, a slat-board bed, and in one corner a chamber pot, which he carried out every morning himself.

I slept in a room on the other side of the wall from him. One night after winter had come, I was asleep in my red gown Grandma Hazelton had made for me since we'd come back from Jacksonville, and Mr. Willis' mouth came alive with what had to be an unthinkable pain.

When I heard him kick the slop jar, I knew it was his teeth. I just didn't know right away how bad it was. When the ladder-back chair splintered, I knew it was a bad hurt even for him. A few times that night I managed to slip off to sleep only to be jarred awake when he would run blindly into the thin wall separating us.

He groaned and cursed, not loudly but steadily, sometimes for what seemed like half an hour. Ordinarily, mama would have fixed a hot poultice for his jaw or at least tried to do something. But she had learned he was a proud man and preferred to suffer by himself, especially if it was his teeth bothering him.

The whole house was kept awake most of the night by his thrashing and groaning, by the wash pan being knocked off the shelf, by his broken shaving mirror being broken again, and by his blind charges into the wall.

What was happening was only necessary. The dentist would not have gotten out of his warm bed for anything less than money. And Mr. Willis didn't have any money. Besides, the dentist was in town ten miles away, and we didn't have anything but a wagon and Pete, who, stopping every seventy yards or so to rest, would have taken half a day to get there.

I was huddled under the quilts, shaking with dread, when I heard him kick open the door to his room and thump down the wooden steps in his heavy brogan work shoes, which he had not taken off all night. I couldn't imagine where he was going, but I knew I wanted to watch whatever was about to happen. The only thing worse than my nerves was my curiosity, which had always been untempered by pity or compassion, a serious character failing in most societies but a sanity-saving virtue in Georgia when I was a child.

I went out the front door barefoot onto the frozen ground. I met Mr. Willis coming around the corner of the house. In the dim light I could see the craziness in his eyes, the same craziness you see in the eyes of a trapped fox. Mr. Willis headed straight for the well, with me behind him, shaking in my thin cotton gown. He took the bucket from the nail on the rack built over the open well and sent it shooting down hard as he could to break the inch of ice that was over the water. As he was drawing the bucket up on the pulley, he seemed to see me for the first time.

"What the hell, boy!" he shouted. "What the hell!"

His voice was as mad as his eyes, and he either would not or could not say anything else. He held the bucket and took a mouthful of the freezing water. He held it a long time, spat it out, and filled his mouth again.

He turned the bucket loose and let it fall again into the well instead of hanging it back on the nail where it belonged. With his cheeks swelling with water he took something out of the back pocket of his overalls. As soon as I saw what he had, I knew beyond all belief and good sense what he meant to do, and suddenly I was no longer cold but stood on the frozen ground in a hot passion waiting to *see* him do it, to see if he *could* do it.

He had a piece of croker sack about the size of a half dollar in his left hand and a pair of wire pliers in his right. He spat the water out and reached way back in his rotten mouth and put the piece of sack over a tooth. He braced his feet against the well and stuck the pliers in over the sackcloth. He took the pliers in both hands, and immediately a forked vein leaped in his forehead. The vein in his neck popped big as a pencil. He pulled and twisted and pulled and never made a sound.

It took him a long time, and finally, as he fought with the pliers and with himself, his braced feet slipped so that he was flat on his back when the blood broke from his mouth, followed by the pliers holding a tooth with roots half an inch long. He got slowly to his feet, sweat running on his face, and held the bloody tooth up between us.

He looked at the tooth and said in his old, calm, recognizable voice: "Hurt now, you sumbitch!"

His old teeth never hurt him again like that while he was with us. They hurt him bad enough to make him stomp around and break a few things, but never bad enough again to make him go into his mouth with a pair of pliers. And it was just as well, too, because things were dreadful enough without that. But he never complained as he kept his methodical but incredibly slow pace fixing up the fence to keep the stock out (we didn't have any to keep *in*), and putting in a big patch of collards and turnips—a winter garden that doesn't even taste really good until the first frost has fallen on them—and building a pen for the hundred tiny biddies ordered by mama and brought by the mailman.

After we got the biddies, my grandma came to live with us. She woke up one morning paralyzed in her leg and arm and the cheek of her face, so they hauled her over to us in a pickup truck. Uncle Alton took in grandpa, who had withdrawn more and more into the silence of deafness. He spent his days reading three newspapers and taking little sips of moonshine from a jar on the mantelshelf. Grandma rocked relentlessly, stared into the middle distance a lot, and drained her mouth of snuff into a can beside her chair. But she took what came her way without complaining. Her mind was alert and she liked to talk. We were all glad she was with us except that the house was not big enough to accommodate another child, much less an old crippled lady. She didn't eat as much as a bird, but we didn't have enough extra food to feed a bird, not even a small one. Hunger was already in the house when she got there. But we made do.

We were already beginning to go out to the pen Mr. Willis built and stare at the biddies. They were then about as big as good-sized sparrows. Each day we tried to calculate how much longer it would be before we could fry up some.

"We could do six, even ten," my brother said.

"Not now," mama said.

"They big as dove, some of'm," I said.

"But they ain't dove," she said. "They biddies."

"I reckon," said Mr. Willis. "Howsomever, I have seen'm split down the middle and cooked in two pieces."

It was late afternoon and we were standing in the backyard. Even Grandma Hazelton. She carried her paralyzed hand in a sling from her neck and leaned heavily on a walking stick she held in her good hand. If she took her time, she got around pretty well in a kind of sliding, sidewise shuffle, dragging her bad leg. She had been helped down the steps when she came out with us to look at the biddies.

Just as we were about to go back in, a red-tailed chicken hawk glided low and fast over where we stood, taking a good look for himself into the pen.

"We gone have to git that hawk," she said. "Don't won't none of us be eating them biddies." She looked at me and winked her good eye. "You and me'll fix that gentleman to-morrow."

Mr. Willis said: "I don't believe it's a gun on the place."

"Won't need one," said Grandma Hazelton, turning to begin the long, slow shuffle back to her rocking chair.

She woke me up early the next morning. "We better git on out there an fix breakfast for that hawk," she said.

I got out of bed and, still wearing my gown, let her shuffle on down the hall to the backyard. She allowed me to help her down the three wooden steps, that being the only help she would accept. We went on back to the pen and stood looking in.

Chickens, as everybody knows, are cannibals. Let a biddy get a spot of blood on it from a scrape or a raw place and the other biddies will simply eat it alive.

"Git me that one out," she said, pointing. "The one bout half eat up."

I brought it to her. It was scabby, practically featherless, with one wing nearly pecked away. She took it into her old soft, liver-colored hands and stroked its head gently with her thumb until it settled down. Then she opened one of her snuff cans, and I saw it was a quarter full of arsenic. Calmly and with great care, she covered the biddy's head and raw neck, making sure none of the poison got in its eyes.

She handed it to me. "Put it out yonder by the fence. If it don't stay there, we'll have to tie it down with a string the hawk can break."

The biddy stayed where I put it though; it had been too brutalized by the other biddies in the pen to have much inclination to move around. And it wasn't long—still early morning—before the hawk came in low over the fence, its red tail fanned, talons stretched, and nailed the poisoned biddy where it squatted in the dust. The biddy never made a sound as it was carried away. My gentle crippled grandma watched it all with satisfaction. The hawk lit in a tree in a head of woods, and I could plainly see him tearing at the biddy on the limb.

I loved the old lady for all things she showed me and told me, but the time came when she got in the way of what I wanted to do, and I showed my true, little-boy colors. Mama had to go to Waycross, which was an overnight trip. Mr. Willis took the opportunity to visit some of his own connections over in Jeff Davis County. That left my brother and me to look after grandma and take care of things on the place. Mama cooked us some food and left it in the safe, and then caught a ride to town, where she could get the bus for Waycross. She told us to clean up after we ate—wash the dishes, put the food back in the stove—and, above all, not to leave the spoon in the gravy.

"You leave that spoon in the gravy and it'll be ruint sure. Taste just like tin."

She caught her ride, and everything went fine that first day until about sundown, when Ray came over on the mule. Ray was a friend of my brother's who lived on the next farm. He was going down the creek for some catfish and wanted us to come with him. My brother was all for it, and of course, I was too. But that left a problem. Grandma. I told her she'd be all right. She said she wouldn't.

"I'm scared," she said. "Don't leave me here all by myself."

"You'll have to stay," my brother said to me.

Who else? I was the youngest, and if anybody was going to stay home and do something dull and boring like look after an old crippled lady, it would have to be me.

"I don't want to," I said.

"She's scared," he said.

"Tell'm you ain't scared," I said. "If you don't, they gone make me stay."

"I'm scared," she said. They made me stay.

They made me stay, but as soon as they were gone, I started closing up the house, every door, every window.

"What you doing, son?"

I'd gone into a little room where she was lying down and where my own narrow bed was jammed into one corner. It was just getting on toward dark on one of those occasionally steaming days Bacon County sometimes has in late September just before it begins to cool into fall.

"I locked up everything," I said. "It's so many bad things out there in the dark, you cain't tell what's apt to come in here and git us."

Her old washed blue eyes watched me steadily in the light from a kerosene lamp I'd lighted on the little table beside her bed. She smiled uncertainly. "Ah, son," she said.

The room was tight and hot and smelled of dust. The liver

spots grew almost black in her ivory skin, and sweat started on her thin blue temples.

"Please, son, please, a little air," she said. "Cain't we open one winder?"

"I think we better keep them winders closed," I said, "so we won't be scared."

I kept the dear old lady sweating, locked there in that steaming room, until my brother came back about four hours later. He immediately wanted to know what was going on. I told him. He, always being much more gentle-natured and decent than I, was not sympathetic.

"Boy, you gone git you tail beat bad when mama gits home."

I had already known that when I started shutting the house up. We both assumed grandma would tell on me, and maybe she would have if things had been different.

When mama got home the next day and went back to the kitchen, the first thing she saw was that gravy bowl. It had a spoon in it. My brother and I had followed her back to the kitchen, and we saw the spoon the same time she saw it. Both of us kind of hunkered down, shriveled where we stood. Grandma was in her chair between the back door and the wood stove and saw it all.

Mama turned slowly from the safe, her eyes blazing, and said in a calm, flat, terrible voice: "You the two sorriest boys that ever shit out of the gills of an asshole."

The skin over my heart went cold, and I could already feel the viselike knees gripping my head. But it was not to happen.

"These boys been just as good as they could," grandma said. "They taken precious care of me." She was looking directly at me where I stood, guilt pouring over me like scalding water. "They *both* taken precious care of me."

I went to bed that night a very different boy than I had ever been before. Or at least with a different understanding than I had before. I don't know how much it affected whatever I've done since, but that moment between mama and grandma and me was fixed forever in my head and heart as if nailed there.

CHAPTER 12

During that year, partly because grandma was staying with us, I began to think of Uncle Alton as if he were my daddy. He had been keeping grandpa ever since grandma had her stroke and the old folks had to break up housekeeping. Uncle Alton would come down to our place to see his mama, and sometimes he would take grandma up to his place so she could get together with grandpa for a while.

From the beginning I loved him and wanted to be near him. It was never anything he said to me, but rather the way he treated me. He never treated me like I was a stump, as other poeple seemed to do. He noticed me. He acted like I might be somebody good to have around, somebody who could help a man with a job.

The first time I ever went cooning in Little Satilla River, he took me. I knew about cooning, but I'd never done it. And I was scared to death. Cooning is catching fish with your hands in the shallow sloughs off the river where the banks are a tangle of roots. You stick your hands up in the roots and trap fish there.

The notion of sticking my hands underwater and up into pockets of roots where I could not see made the hair get up on my neck. But if he noticed my fear, he never mentioned it.

"Git down here beside me, son," he said, "and help me with this fish. We got to be careful, though. I think it's a catfish. Mind you don't git finned."

He was waist deep in the creek, and I got in with him, up to my shoulders. The feel of his arm around my shoulders, and him saying *we* had to be careful, made me so happy I cried. He thought I had snagged a finger on a root, and I let him think it. The truth was, at that moment, I would have stuck my *head* under the water and into the roots if he had asked me to.

He took me squirrel hunting the first time I ever went, and he let me use his gun. He showed me how to whittle a trigger for a rabbit trap made out of a hollow log. He told me why the hair must not touch the meat when a goat is being skinned, and then showed me how to do it. But perhaps the best thing he ever showed me—made me *feel*—was that a man does not back away from doing whatever is necessary, no matter how unpleasant.

Our biddies were about half as big as a pigeon when the rooster began to get sluggish, walking about the yard with his head and tail feathers drooping. Everybody had noticed it— Mr. Willis first mentioned it—but Uncle Alton was the first to do something about it. He and I were on the porch with grandma, she in her chair, we on the doorsteps when the rooster came moping around the corner of the house.

"Alton," she said, "you ought to do sumpin about that rooster. He's lookin like, mama, I've come home to die."

"He ain't gone die, ma," he said.

"Will you don't do something?"

"I reckon Harry and me's gone help'm a little."

"You know what ails'm?"

"Yes, ma'am, I reckon I do."

That was another thing, which I understand imperfectly to this day: how mysteriously wonderful it was to be around Uncle Alton when he was with *his* mama. Here was a man old enough to be my daddy, and who I wished was my daddy, saying "Yes, ma'am," to his mama just like I said, "Yes, ma'am" to mine. With my life as broken, tenuous, and imperiled on every side as it seemed, knowing that we were the same blood, knowing that the blood went from that gentle, ruined old lady to Uncle Alton to me made me feel less alone, less helpless.

"Go over there and pick'm up, son," Uncle Alton said. "I don't reckon he's gone run much. I'll go in and git a few things from Myrtice."

Mama had the stove going, and so there was hot water in

the reservoir. Along with the hot water, Uncle Alton found some turpentine, the only sterilizing agent we had, and some clean rags to wipe the turpentine off before it could blister, and some fishing line and a long curving needle used to repair harness. He brought it all out on the front porch, where I was holding the sick rooster. My brother was in the field with Mr. Willis, and mama, as soon as she found out what was going on, wanted no part of it. I kept calling for her to come and look while we worked, but she stayed in the kitchen.

"Now what it is, son," said Uncle Alton, when he had everything ready, "is he's crawbound. Feel right here." He took my hand and put it at the base of the rooster's neck. As young as I was, I had felt enough chickens' craws to know something was wrong. The rooster's was tight and solid as stone. "He'll be dead in a few days, maybe even tomorrow if we don't help'm. We got to clean out that craw."

I held the rooster on his back, and Uncle Alton cleaned the feathers off his craw and then shaved him down with his razor-sharp castrating knife, a spot about as big as a lemon. The rooster was too sick to care. But when Uncle Alton sliced open his craw, the rooster screamed with a sound a child might have made. Feathers and blood stuck to my hands. The thin, shivering body pulsed under my fingers. Uncle Alton was quick, and in his quickness showed every trust and confidence in me. It was a horrible and beautiful moment.

"Cut in a little deeper there, son," said grandma.

"Yes, ma'am," said Uncle Alton. "Son, git that turpentine swab right here."

"Yes, sir."

"Clean it down in the corner, Alton."

"Yes, ma'am," said Uncle Alton. "Son, I got the needle started, but I cain't git the end of it. See if you can."

"Yes, sir," I said. Uncle Alton's hand moved to take the rooster's feet, and my own fingers were suddenly deep in the wound, the living flesh slipping and throbbing.

The rooster lived to get his share of the biddies growing up in the pen back of the house. I never saw him walking around the yard that I did not remember that his blood had been on my fingers, and more, that I had touched his blood because Uncle Alton had treated me like a son he trusted. Just knowing Uncle Alton was in the world helped me deal with what was ahead of me that year.

What was ahead of me was God and little girls. The mystery and general scariness of both. As the year moved into winter, I went to wood sawings and peanut poppings for the first time. Families gathered all over Bacon County to saw logs that would be used to cook tobacco the following summer and to shell peanuts for seed. A farmer snaked up as many logs as he could cut, and then the night of the party all the men and the young bucks sipped a little moonshine and sawed themselves into a sweat. Sometimes eight or ten crosscut saws would be working at the same time, steam rising off the men's bodies in the cold air, their straining faces lighted by an enormous bonfire. Sometime later in the evening, a fiddler started and the sawing stopped. Peanut poppings were the same kind of party. A farmer would have saved back sacks of peanuts from the year before. If he wanted to plant ten or fifteen acres, an incredible number of peanuts had to be shelled by hand. Thirty-five or forty people, men, women, and children, sat around for three or four hours with peanuts in their laps, shelling as fast as they could. Finally, somebody began pushing furniture back and the first tentative squawks of the fiddle cut through the cold night air.

But mostly what went on at these parties was *walking out*. Walking out means just what it says: boys and girls walked out together into the darkness. They walked down the lane holding hands, and in a few minutes they came back, only to walk out again in a little bit. The mothers kept careful track of their daughters, how long they'd been out with a boy, and if a girl had been gone more than five or ten minutes, a mother might go sailing out into the dark, her apron flapping, to find her.

But for a child less than ten years old, walking out wasn't necessary. You could go at it in the backyard or anywhere, because nobody paid any attention to you. Perhaps that is why there was such tremendous pressure to do *it* and, consequently, a lot of hot, smarmy struggling of little, bony bodies in dark places about the house and the farm.

There was a boy my age named Bonehead whom I had got to be friends with at school who was forever at me to do *it*. A great many others were pushing me about the same thing, but Bonehead was the worst.

"You git any, boy?"

"Naw. I just about did, but I didn't."

"You got to git yoursef some."

"I know," I said, in real dejection. "I know I do."

I knew that I did, that sooner or later I'd be minding my own business in some dark corner of the farmhouse or out in the lane and Bonehead would turn up with a little girl who had *it*, and there I'd be. I knew the details of the thing. Hadn't my brother explained it all and got me under the house with Lottie Mae? Hadn't I seen jacks and mares, bulls and cows banging away at each other? So I knew I had to get myself some, but the problem was that I didn't want any.

As long as I thought about cows and bulls, or even men and women, I was all right. But when I thought about *me* and. . . . Clearly impossible. I had lots of little girls down on their backs in Springfield Section of Jacksonville, and it was fun—a little like wrestling—until it got too feverish. Then I would jump up and run.

The mystery of little girls stood at dead even with the mystery of God. See, little girls had *it*. None of the little boys had *it*. We had to go through all kinds of things—fights, gifts, lies, whatever—if we wanted *it*. And little girls could give us some of *it* if they wanted to. As well as being unpleasant, the whole thing was scary.

But then we had an evangelist come to the county to preach, and everything was all rolled into the same ball. Obviously, there was no walking out at church, but the boys and girls managed. At night services, they *did* manage. I don't know why it was so. But after the last service at night, if you could have heard the hymens popping it would have sounded like crickets in a field.

Bonehead was sitting on the aisle seat. I was next to him and pressed in on me from the other side was a boy named Alonzo. We were huddled in the Baptist Church, driven there by our parents against our wills, knowing what we were going to find.

Our own minister had prepared us for the evangelist, a man from Colorado, who continuously traveled about the country calling down the Wrath of the Living God on all unsaved heads. He also called down the Love, which sounded exactly like the Wrath, of the Living God on the same heads.

Hell came right along with God, hand in hand. The stink of sulfur swirled in the air of the church, fire burned in the aisles, and brimstone rained out of the rafters. From the evangelist's oven mouth spewed images of a place with pitchforks, and devils, and lakes of fire that burned forever. God had fixed a place like that because he loved us so much.

With a God like that on one side and a hell like that on the other, it was enough to make a little boy unaware of his loosening bowels, but even when I realized, I didn't care. What was filling my shoes compared to a God who might boil me *forever* (a word and a condition I could not imagine)? Worse, He was going to do it for reasons of love. He had—the evangelist said—sent His only son to be beaten with brambles and given vinegar to drink and finally even nailed to a tree for the same reasons of love.

I couldn't imagine such a being. But that didn't help a bit. It gave no comfort at all, because by now the man raging up there in the pulpit owned me, every cell—blood, bone, and hair. Faith had nothing to do with it. I was one with the voice and the vision of the God-crazed evangelist, standing six and a half feet tall in cowboy boots, joyous in his anger at my filthy life, with hands so enormous that as he buried me in the water later that night, his fingers wrapped my head as if it were an orange.

When a man like that told you God, by God, was coming soon, was probably on His way this very night to touch you with His Love if you didn't *come on home to Jesus right now!*

you didn't argue about it, resist it, or even think about it. You just shit in your pants, stood up and staggered down the aisle toward the altar, blinded by tears and terror.

But I had always known I would someday have to do God. I had been watching people do Him all my life: fainting, screaming, crying, and thrashing about over the floor. My turn had come and I'd survived him. All that was left was *it* as I charged out into the night. I don't remember what I was thinking or if I was thinking anything. But as Bonehead kept watch for the little girl's older sister, whom their mother had sent to look for her, I got a little girl down on the dark back porch of the church, delirious, full of God and raging. I didn't know when it was over if she had given me *it* or not. But Bonehead and I were both pretty sure she had. She was crying because not only had I ripped her little cotton drawers, but I had thrown them in the yard and she didn't know what she was going to tell her mama.

For my part it was a great relief, getting on the right side of God and little girls all in the same hour. I went back to the farm that night and slept the sleep of one who is at peace with the world. It carried me nicely through the year while the turnips and collards grew green and marvelous in the winter and died in the spring, while the biddies grew up and scratched around in the yard with the rooster, and while Pete got another year grayer, another year slower.

From the beginning, though, I wanted somebody to tell about the girl and God, somebody grown. I don't know why I wanted to tell a grownup, maybe only to have what I had done confirmed as fine. Whatever the reason, as the weeks and months went by, the desire to tell somebody got stronger. I was no longer as certain as I had been. I wasn't sleeping as well. I woke up in the yard and in the fields more often sleepwalking.

Then the chance came. Mr. Willis was going to take corn to town to be ground at the mill into grits and meal. It was a sunup-to-after-dark trip, and I was allowed to go with him. We shelled out the corn, put Pete between the shaves, and eased out onto the road to Alma while it was still dark.

We were hardly out of sight of the house when I told Mr. Willis the whole story of God and the girl. It was a slow and tortuous telling. But it was easy enough to do. The burden had become too great to keep to myself. I was beginning to think that the girl had canceled out God. You don't git *it* from Him and run around to His back porch and git *it* from a girl. If in fact I had got *it* from either of them. I was no longer very sure.

Mr. Willis sat in a ladder-back chair in the bed of the wagon, looking straight ahead, while I told him all of it. The sun showed full above the wall of black pine trees when I finally finished.

He sighed and said matter-of-factly: "God an girls is just like farmin. You cain't ever git finished. Take sumpin out of the ground and it's time to put sumpin in again. Soon's you find out you ain't never gone git finished, you don't have to hurry or worry." He sent a long stream of tobacco juice over the traces. "If the grass is growing or *not* growing ain't sumpin a reasonable man oughta worry about. The grass is *gone* grow."

I didn't know what to say to him, so I said: "It's gone take a long time to git where we going."

He looked out over Pete's aged, bony withers and said: "Oh, it *always* takes a long time to git where you going."

In July of 1956 I was standing at the edge of a tobacco field with four of my cousins waiting for the sled to come from the barn. The month before I had been discharged from the Marine Corps after serving three years. I'd come back to Bacon County to visit my kin people. I had no plans to return to Georgia to live, although I thought someday I probably would. Thus far, twenty-two years later, I never have. But on that sweltering day in July, standing in the tobacco field, it felt as though I had never left. It felt good to be home again.

We'd worked since before daylight, cropping tobacco so it could be sledded to the barn where the leaves would be strung onto sticks and put into the barn to cook. My cousins were about my age, boys I'd grown up with, and as close to me as brothers. We'd had a good time that day working, although it had been hard, dusty, and hot. Particularly hot. It was early afternoon now, and I could feel the sun across my shoulders, where it lay like a weight.

The sled we'd been waiting for turned into the field. It was time to stoop to the stalks again, time to go between the rows of tobacco where no breeze ever reached. My cousins had been kidding me all day about getting bear-caught, by which they meant that I would probably go down from exhaustion and heat before we finished the field. And they were closer to the truth than they knew. Three years in the Marine Corps had not prepared me for a Georgia summer in a tobacco patch.

Looking at me, Edward said: "Boy, I believe I see the bear out yonder behind a tree."

"I believe he wants *you*," his brother Roger said, smiling.

The youngest boy, Jones, looked out into the woods bordering the field. "I believe he means to come in here and git on your back."

It had all got a little beyond joking to me, because I didn't know if I was going to make the rest of the day or not. I glanced up at the sky and said: "Goddamn sun."

As soon as I'd spoken, I knew what I had done. The four boys preceptibly flinched. When they turned to look at me, the joking and laughter were gone.

"Look," I said, "I . . . I didn't. . . ."

But there was nothing I could say. I had already done what, in Bacon County, was unthinkable. I had cursed the sun. And in Bacon County you don't curse the sun or the rain or the land or God. They are all the same thing. To curse any of them is an ultimate blasphemy. I had known that three years ago, but in three years I had somehow managed to forget it. I stood there feeling how much I had left this place and these people, and at the same time knowing that it would be forever impossible to leave them completely. Wherever I might go in the world, they would go with me.

The Gospel Singer

In Crews's first novel published in 1968, a gifted singer returns to his poor hometown and a life and family he now holds in contempt. *The Gospel Singer* reveals the absurdity of blind religious faith and idol worship, and the hypocrisy that results with the offering of money or sex. This darkly comic, bitingly satirical novel displays Crews's brilliant literary talent that garnered critical acclaim and a cult following.

"Harry Crews is magnificently twisted and brutally funny."
— Carl Hiaasen